Dealing with Emotional Problems Using Rational Emotive Behaviour Therapy (REBT): A Client's Guide

The second edition of *Dealing with Emotional Problems Using Rational Emotive Behaviour Therapy (REBT): A Client's Guide* offers clear, practical advice on how to deal with some of the most common emotional difficulties we face.

Rational Emotive Behaviour Therapy (REBT) is a therapy approach that encourages a direct focus on emotional problems, helping you to understand the attitudes, thoughts and behaviours that lead you to maintain these problems. This understanding will enable you to overcome problems and lead a happier and more fulfilling life. The book begins by outlining foundations of emotional problems. Each problem is then presented in a similar way, allowing the reader to compare and contrast similarities and differences between each emotion, and teaching them how to cope with it.

This book covers:

- anxiety
- depression
- guilt
- shame
- hurt
- unhealthy anger
- unhealthy jealousy
- unhealthy envy
- and a new chapter on unhealthy regret.

Featuring newly revised information and language on REBT, this *Client's Guide* is an accessible, user-friendly guide that can be used on your own or in conjunction with a therapist who can use the *Practitioner's Guide*.

Windy Dryden is in clinical and consultative practice and is an international authority on Single-Session Therapy. He is Emeritus Professor of Psychotherapeutic Studies at Goldsmiths University of London. He has worked in psychotherapy for more than 45 years and is the author or editor of over 265 books.

Dealing with Emotional Problems Using Rational Emotive Behaviour Therapy (REBT)

A Client's Guide

Second Edition

WINDY DRYDEN

Routledge
Taylor & Francis Group

LONDON AND NEW YORK

Designed cover image: © Getty Images

Second edition published 2024
by Routledge
4 Park Square, Milton Park, Abingdon, Oxon, OX14 4RN

and by Routledge
605 Third Avenue, New York, NY 10158

Routledge is an imprint of the Taylor & Francis Group, an informa business

© 2024 Windy Dryden

The right of Windy Dryden to be identified as author of this work has been asserted in accordance with sections 77 and 78 of the Copyright, Designs and Patents Act 1988.

First edition published by Routledge 2012

British Library Cataloguing-in-Publication Data
A catalogue record for this book is available from the British Library

Library of Congress Cataloging-in-Publication Data
Names: Dryden, Windy, author.
Title: Dealing with emotional problems using rational emotive behaviour therapy (REBT) : a client's guide / Windy Dryden.
Other titles: Dealing with emotional problems using rational-emotive cognitive behaviour therapy. Client's guide
Description: Second edition. | Milton Park, Abingdon, Oxon ; New York, NY : Routledge, 2024. | Revised edition of: Dealing with emotional problems using rational-emotive cognitive behaviour therapy. c2012. | Includes bibliographical references and index.
Identifiers: LCCN 2023025208 (print) | LCCN 2023025209 (ebook) | ISBN 9781032543239 (hardback) | ISBN 9781032542539 (paperback) | ISBN 9781003424307 (ebook)
Subjects: LCSH: Rational emotive behavior therapy. | Cognitive therapy.
Classification: LCC RC489.R3 D7863 2024 (print) | LCC RC489.R3 (ebook) | DDC 616.89/1425–dc23/eng/20230831
LC record available at https://lccn.loc.gov/2023025208
LC ebook record available at https://lccn.loc.gov/2023025209

ISBN: 9781032543239 (hbk)
ISBN: 9781032542539 (pbk)
ISBN: 9781003424307 (ebk)

DOI: 10.4324/9781003424307

Typeset in Stone Serif
by Newgen Publishing UK

Contents

Preface

In this book, I am going to cover the nine emotional problems that people routinely seek help for and how you can deal with them. I wanted to discuss all nine problems in one volume, since many of you will experience more than one such emotional problem during your lives.

I begin the book by outlining the foundations of the emotional problems. I then devote one chapter to each of the nine emotional problems and use a similar structure in each chapter. Thus, I start by helping you to understand the emotional problem in question, discuss what you disturb yourself about when you experience the emotion, and outline what largely determines the emotion and how you tend to act and think when you experience it. Then, I discuss how you can deal with the emotional problem in question. I will help you to identify the themes in the emotion, and your behaviour and thinking when you experience it, before encouraging you to set appropriate emotional, behavioural and thinking goals. Then, I will help you to identify, examine and change the rigid/extreme attitudes that account for your emotional problem and to develop the flexible and non-extreme attitudes that will enable you to achieve your goals. Next, I show you what you need to do to strengthen your conviction in your flexible and non-extreme attitudes so that you become less prone to your emotional problem. I then deal with a number of additional issues relevant to the emotional problem in question, before finally outlining a number of world views that underpin the emotional problem and its healthy alternative.

The common chapter structure that I employ in Chapters 2–10 is to ensure that all relevant issues are discussed for each emotional problem. It is unlikely that you will be prone to all eight emotional problems, but you may be prone to two or three. The view of emotional problems that I am taking in this book states that, while there are common features among the eight emotions, there are also features that are distinctive to each emotion. This is reflected in Chapters 2–10 and you will need to bear this point in mind when you read these chapters (or a selection of them).

You can use this guide on its own or in conjunction with therapy. If you have a therapist, I have written a *Practitioner's Guide* companion volume to help your therapist help you to get the most out of this book.

Windy Dryden
London and Eastbourne

Emotional problems: foundations and healthy alternatives

In this book, I am going to discuss some common emotional problems and show you how to deal with them. The book is structured as a workbook so that you can implement the skills that I teach you in a step-by-step manner.

In this opening chapter, I am going to cover some important material that I regard as foundations to your understanding of the nine emotional problems that I discuss in this book and their healthy alternatives.

WHAT ARE THE NINE EMOTIONAL PROBLEMS?

I have been practising in the field of counselling and psychotherapy since 1975 and have worked in a variety of different settings. In that time, I have seen many people suffering from one or more of the nine emotional problems that I cover in this book. They are:

- anxiety
- depression
- guilt
- unhealthy regret
- shame
- hurt
- unhealthy anger
- unhealthy jealousy
- unhealthy envy.

You will note that I have put the adjective 'unhealthy' in front of regret, anger, jealousy and envy. I have done this to distinguish the unhealthy version of the emotion from its healthy version. I will discuss healthy alternatives to the nine emotional problems in the next section.

DOI: 10.4324/9781003424307-1

HEALTHY ALTERNATIVES TO THE NINE EMOTIONAL PROBLEMS

Adversity is unfortunately a fact of life.[1] None of us can say that we have lived a life untouched by adversity. An adversity is a negative event. So when you are looking for a healthy alternative to an emotional problem in the face of adversity, it is not realistic for you to select an emotion that is positive or neutral.

Problems with positive emotions as healthy alternatives to the emotional problems

If you want to feel a positive emotion about an adversity, you will have to convince yourself that it is good that the adversity happened. Now, I concede that adversities do have some positive features, but they are largely negative in nature. As such, the only way you are going to convince yourself that it is a good thing that an adversity happened is to lie to yourself and to believe your lie. As you can see, this is unlikely to work in the longer term and is, thus, not a good strategy.

Problems with neutral emotions as healthy alternatives to the emotional problems

It is also not realistic to have a neutral feeling about an adversity. If you want such a neutral response, you will have to convince yourself that it does not matter to you that the adversity happened. However, that won't work since it does matter to you that the adversity happened. Quite properly, you would have preferred that the adversity did not happen. So again the only way you are going to convince yourself that it doesn't matter to you that the adversity happened is to lie to yourself and to find your lie convincing. This, again, is unlikely to work in the longer term and is, thus, not a good strategy.

Problems with living in an emotional vacuum as a healthy alternative to the emotional problems

If a positive or neutral emotional response to an adversity is ruled out as a healthy alternative to an emotional problem, what is left? You could say that, when an adversity happens, you don't want to feel the emotional problem that you felt.

> Harry regularly experiences anxiety about going to see his tutor because he thinks she is going to criticise his work. When asked what he wanted to feel instead, Harry replied: 'I don't want to be anxious about the possibility of my tutor criticising my work.'

The problem with this approach is that we don't tend to live in an emotional vacuum when an adversity has happened or we think that it is likely to happen. Thus, it matters to Harry that his tutor does not criticise him. We experience emotions in areas of life that matter to us. Since it matters to Harry that his tutor does not criticise him, he is going to experience an emotion about this prospect. Don't forget that we are looking for a healthy alternative to the emotional problem of anxiety in Harry's case, and to all nine emotional problems in general.

Problems with reducing the intensity of emotional problems as healthy alternatives to these emotional problems

People often say when they are asked to nominate a healthy alternative to an emotional problem that they want to feel a less intense version of the emotional problem. Applying this to our example, when asked what he wants to feel instead of anxiety about seeing his tutor, Harry says that he wants to feel less anxious. Now the problem with having a less intense version of an emotional problem as a healthy alternative for that emotion is that it is still unhealthy, albeit less intense. If something is unhealthy, it would make sense to want to have a less intense version of it only if this is the only alternative available. Fortunately, it isn't!

Healthy negative emotions (HNEs) as healthy alternatives to the emotional problems

Healthy alternatives to emotional problems are known as 'healthy negative emotions' (HNEs). This term is used for two good reasons. First, such emotions have a negative tone and this is their realistic aspect.

Remember we are talking about emotions in the context of life's adversities. It is realistic to feel a negative emotion about a negative event. Second, such emotions are healthy in that they are associated with a different set of behaviours and ways of thinking than are emotional problems. I discuss this in greater detail later in this chapter. For now, here is the list of HNEs:[2]

- concern (rather than anxiety)

- sadness (rather than depression)

- remorse (rather than guilt)

- healthy regret (rather than unhealthy regret)

- disappointment (rather than shame)

- sorrow (rather than hurt)

- healthy anger (rather than unhealthy anger)

- healthy jealousy (rather than unhealthy jealousy)

- healthy envy (rather than unhealthy envy).

RATIONAL EMOTIVE BEHAVIOUR THERAPY

This book is based on Rational Emotive Behaviour Therapy (known as REBT). You may have heard of cognitive behaviour therapy (CBT) and it being described as a therapeutic approach. However, in my view, CBT is not a therapeutic approach, but a therapeutic tradition in which there are a number of distinctive approaches, of which REBT is one. REBT was founded in 1955 by Dr Albert Ellis (1913–2007).

The nine emotional problems are underpinned by rigid/extreme attitudes

REBT theory argues that each of the nine emotional problems stems from a rigid attitude and one or more of three extreme attitudes that are derived from the rigid attitude. Apart from being rigid and extreme, these attitudes have three other characteristics:

⊙ They are false.

⊙ They are illogical.

⊙ They have largely unconstructive consequences (e.g., in the face of an adversity they lead to emotional problems).

Let me consider rigid and extreme attitudes separately.

Rigid attitudes

Perhaps the most basic characteristic of human beings is that we have desires. We want certain things to happen and other things not to happen, but when we turn these desires into rigidities when we don't get what we want, or get what we don't want, then we experience one or more of the emotional problems described in this book. Here are a few examples of rigid attitudes:

⊙ I must do well on the forthcoming test.

⊙ You must respect my boundaries.

⊙ The world must not give me too much hassle.

As these examples show, you can hold rigid attitudes towards yourself, others and life conditions.

Three extreme attitudes

According to REBT theory, rigid attitudes are paramount in explaining the existence of the emotional problems. Three extreme attitudes tend to be derived from these rigid attitudes. These are:

⊙ awfulising attitudes;

⊙ unbearability attitudes; and

⊙ devaluation attitudes.

Awfulising attitudes

An awfulising attitude from the rigid attitude that things must not be as bad as they are. An awfulising attitude is extreme in the sense that you hold *at the time* one or more of the following:

⊙ Nothing could be worse.

⊚ The event in question is worse than 100 per cent bad.

⊚ No good could possibly come from this bad event.

⊚ It is not possible for me to get over this event.

In the following examples of awfulising attitudes, the rigid attitudes are listed in parentheses:

⊚ (I must do well on the forthcoming test)… and it will be awful if I don't.

⊚ (You must respect my boundaries)… and it's the end of the world when you don't.

⊚ (The world must not give me too much hassle)… and it's terrible when it does.

Unbearability attitudes

An unbearability attitude stems from a rigid attitude that things must not be as frustrating or uncomfortable as they are. An unbearability attitude is extreme in the sense that you hold *at the time* one or more of the following:

⊚ I will die or disintegrate if the adversity I am facing continues to exist.

⊚ I will lose the capacity to experience happiness if the adversity I am facing continues to exist.

In the following examples of unbearability attitudes, the rigid attitudes are listed in parentheses:

⊚ (I must do well on the forthcoming test)… and I could not bear it if I don't.

⊚ (You must respect my boundaries)… and it's intolerable if you don't.

⊚ (The world must not give me too much hassle)… and I can't stand it if it does.

Devaluation attitudes

A devaluation attitude stems from the rigid attitude that you, others or things must be as you want them to be and is extreme in the sense that you hold *at the time* one or more of the following:

- A person (self or other) can legitimately be given a single global rating that defines their essence and the worth of a person is dependent upon conditions that change (e.g., my worth goes up when I do well and goes down when I don't do well).

- The world can legitimately be given a single rating that defines its essential nature and the value of the world varies according to what happens within it (e.g., the value of the world goes up when something fair occurs and goes down when something unfair happens).

- A person can be rated on the basis of one of his or her aspects and the world can be rated on the basis of one of its aspects.

In the following examples of devaluation attitudes, the rigid attitudes are listed in parentheses:

- (I must do well on the forthcoming test)… and I am a failure if I don't.

- (You must respect my boundaries)… and you are bad if you don't.

- (The world must not give me too much hassle)… and, if it does, the world is a rotten place.

The healthy alternatives to the nine emotional problems are underpinned by flexible and non-extreme attitudes

REBT theory argues that each of the nine healthy alternatives to the emotional problems stems from a flexible attitude and one or more of three non-extreme attitudes that are derived from the flexible attitude. Apart from being flexible and non-extreme, these attitudes have three other characteristics:

- They are true.

- They are logical.

- They have largely constructive consequences (e.g., in the face of an adversity they lead to an HNE).

Let me consider flexible and non-extreme attitudes separately.

Flexible attitudes

As I pointed out earlier in this chapter, it is a basic characteristic of human beings that we have desires. We want certain things to happen and other things not to happen. When we keep these desires flexible and we don't get what we want, or get what we don't want, we experience one or more of the HNEs outlined earlier. Here are a few examples of flexible attitudes:

- I would like to do well on the forthcoming test, but I don't have to do so.
- I want you to respect my boundaries, but unfortunately you don't have to do so.
- I would prefer it if the world did not give me too much hassle, but the world does not have to be the way I want it to be.

As these examples show, you can hold flexible attitudes towards yourself, others and life conditions. You will note from these examples that flexible attitudes have two components:

- an 'asserted preference' component (e.g., 'I would like to do well on the forthcoming test...'); and
- a 'negated rigid' component (e.g., '... but I don't have to do so').

Three non-extreme attitudes

According to REBT theory, flexible attitudes are paramount in explaining the existence of HNEs and three non-extreme attitudes tend to be derived from these flexible attitudes. These are:

- non-awfulising attitudes
- bearability attitudes
- acceptance attitudes.

Non-awfulising attitudes

A non-awfulising attitude stems from the flexible attitude that you would like things not to be as bad as they are, but that doesn't mean that they must not be as bad. This attitude is non-extreme in the sense that you hold *at the time* one or more of the following:

- Things could always be worse.
- The event in question is less than 100 per cent bad.
- Good could come from this bad event.
- It is possible for me to get over this event.

In the following examples of non-awfulising attitudes, the flexible attitudes are listed in parentheses:

- (I would like to do well on the forthcoming test, but I don't have to do so)… and if I don't do well, it would be bad, but not awful.
- (I want you to respect my boundaries, but unfortunately you don't have to do so)… It's disadvantageous to me if you don't, but not the end of the world.
- (I would prefer it if the world did not give me too much hassle, but the world does not have to be the way I want it to be)… It's bad when it's not, but not terrible.

You will note from these examples that non-awfulising attitudes have two components:

- an 'asserted badness' component (e.g., 'If I don't do well on the forthcoming test, it would be bad…'); and
- a 'negated awfulising' component (e.g., '… but it wouldn't be awful').

Bearability attitudes

A bearability attitude stems from the flexible attitude that it is undesirable when adversities are as bad as they are, but unfortunately things don't have to be different. A bearability attitude is non-extreme in the sense that you hold *at the time* one or more of the following:

- I will struggle if the adversity continues to exist, but I will neither die nor disintegrate.

- I will not lose the capacity to experience happiness if the adversity continues to exist, although this capacity will be temporarily diminished.

- The adversity is worth bearing.

- I am worth bearing the adversity for.

- I am willing to bear the adversity.

- I am going to bear the adversity.

In the following examples of bearability attitudes, the flexible attitudes are listed in parentheses:

- (I would like to do well on the forthcoming test, but I don't have to do so)... It will be a struggle for me if I don't do well, but I could bear it and it would be worth bearing. I am worth bearing the adversity for and I am both willing and determined to bear it.

- (I want you to respect my boundaries, but unfortunately you don't have to do so)... It's hard for me to bear it if you don't respect my boundaries, but I can tolerate it and it is in my interests to do so. I am worth bearing this and I am both willing to do so and will do so.

- (I would prefer it if the world did not give me too much hassle, but the world does not have to be the way I want it to be)... When the world is not the way I want, it is difficult me to tolerate it, but I can stand it and it's worthwhile for me to do so and I am worth it too. I am willing to bear the world not being as I want to be and I am committed to do so.

You will note from these examples that bearability attitudes have six components:

- an *asserted struggle* component (e.g., 'It will be a struggle for me if I don't do well on the forthcoming test...');

- a *negated unbearability* component (e.g., ... but I could bear it...');

- an *it's worth it* component (e.g., '... and it would be worth bearing');

- an *I'm worth it* component (e.g., '... and I'm worth bearing it for');

- an *I'm willing to bear it* component (e.g., '... and I am willing to bear it'); and

- an *I'm going to bear it* component (e.g., '... and I am determined to bear it').

Unconditional acceptance attitudes

An unconditional acceptance attitude stems from a flexible attitude that it is preferable, but not necessary, that you, others or things are the way you want them to be and is non-extreme in the sense that you hold *at the time* one or more of the following:

- A person cannot legitimately be given a single global rating that defines their essence, and their worth, as far as they have it, is not dependent upon conditions that change (e.g., my worth stays the same whether or not I do well).

- The world cannot legitimately be given a single rating that defines its essential nature and the value of the world does not vary according to what happens within it (e.g., the value of the world stays the same whether fairness exists at any given time or not).

- It makes sense to rate discrete aspects of a person and of the world, but it does not make sense to rate a person or the world on the basis of these discrete aspects.

In the following examples of unconditional acceptance attitudes, the flexible attitudes are listed in parentheses:

- (I would like to do well on the forthcoming test, but I don't have to do so)... If I don't do well, it's bad, but I am not a failure. I am a unique, unrateable, fallible human being capable of doing well and doing poorly on tests.

- (I want you to respect my boundaries, but unfortunately you don't have to do so)... If you don't, you are not a bad person; rather you are an ordinary human being capable of doing good, bad and neutral things.

- (I would prefer it if the world did not give me too much hassle, but the world does not have to be the way I want it to be)... When the world does give me more hassle than I want, it is not a rotten place; rather it is a complex mixture of good, bad and neutral aspects.

You will note from these examples that unconditional acceptance attitudes have three components:

⦿ an *aspect evaluation* component (e.g., 'If I don't do well, it's bad... ');

⦿ a *negated devaluation* component (e.g., '... but I am not a failure'); and

⦿ an *asserted acceptance* component (e.g., '... I am a unique, unrateable, fallible human being capable of doing well and doing poorly on tests').

INFERENCE THEMES IN RELATION TO YOUR PERSONAL DOMAIN

While emotional problems and HNEs can be differentiated in general by the attitudes that underpin them (rigid and extreme in the first case, flexible and non-extreme in the second), in order to distinguish between particular emotional problems and their specific healthy alternatives, we need to understand a concept known as inference themes, because these relate to an individual's personal domain. Let me discuss the concept of 'personal domain' first.

Personal domain

The concept known as the 'personal domain' first appeared in the psychological literature in 1976 in an excellent book entitled *Cognitive Therapy and the Emotional Disorders* by Dr Aaron T. Beck, one of the grandfathers of CBT. Your personal domain has three features:

⦿ Your personal domain contains people, objects and ideas in which you have an involvement.

⦿ Your personal domain is like an onion in that these people, objects and ideas can occupy a central, intermediate and peripheral place within it.

⦿ There are two basic areas within your personal domain – an ego area and a comfort area. As you will see, seven of the nine emotional problems that I discuss in this book can be related to one or both areas, while two of them (i.e., shame and guilt) appear to be related only to the ego area.

Inference

An inference is an interpretation that you make about a situation that goes beyond the data at hand and one that has personal meaning to you. An inference may be accurate or inaccurate and needs to be tested against the available evidence. Often you do not know for certain if an inference that you have made is accurate or inaccurate and therefore the best you can do is to make the 'best bet' given the data at hand. The accuracy of an inference often becomes clear after you have made it. This is particularly the case when you make an inference about a future event. Let me illustrate these points.

> You will recall that Harry, to whom I referred earlier in this chapter, was anxious about going to see his tutor. If someone asked him what he was anxious about, he would reply 'I am anxious about being criticised by my tutor'. The statement 'being criticised by my tutor' is an inference in that (a) it goes beyond the data at hand; (b) it has personal meaning for Harry; (c) it may be accurate or inaccurate. Whether it is the 'best bet' in the circumstances depends on how critical Harry's tutor is in general.

Inference theme

When Harry made his inference about his tutor's criticism, we know that he felt anxious. When people feel anxious they tend to do so because they infer some kind of threat to their personal domain. Therefore, we can assume that Harry's inference about his tutor's criticism was threat-based. However, we also know that, when people feel concerned (which is the healthy alternative to anxiety), they also tend to do so because they infer some kind of threat to their personal domain. We can conclude from this that, when you make an inference with a threat theme, you will feel either anxious or concerned, but, without knowing anything more, the inference on its own will not help you know whether your emotion is anxiety or concern.

As you will see in the following chapters, when you experience one of the following pairs of emotions, each emotion pairing is related to a specific theme or themes concerned with your personal domain: anxiety vs. concern; depression vs. sadness; guilt vs. remorse; unhealthy regret vs. healthy regret; shame vs. disappointment; hurt vs. sorrow; unhealthy anger vs. healthy anger; unhealthy jealousy vs. healthy jealousy; and unhealthy envy vs. healthy envy. I will discuss and illustrate these themes in the relevant chapters.

DISTINGUISHING EMOTIONAL PROBLEMS FROM THEIR HEALTHY ALTERNATIVES

In this section, I discuss in general how you can reliably distinguish emotional problems from their healthy alternatives. In the chapters that follow I discuss in detail how to distinguish the emotional problem in question with its specific healthy alternative.

Inference themes and attitudes

We know from the above that inference themes show you which of the nine emotional pairings you are experiencing (e.g., when your inference theme is threat, you experience either anxiety or concern), but on their own they do not help you to distinguish which emotion you are experiencing within the pairing (i.e., you cannot tell by the inference theme of threat alone whether your emotion is anxiety or concern).

We also know that, when you hold a rigid/extreme attitude towards an adversity (but we do not know the inference theme of that adversity), your emotion will be unhealthy, but we don't know which of the nine emotional problems you experience. Conversely, we know that, when you hold a flexible/non-extreme attitude towards an adversity (again, we do not know the inference theme of that adversity), your emotion will be a healthy negative one, but again we don't know which of the nine HNEs you experience.

However, when we combine these two bits of information, we are in a better position to distinguish specific emotional problems from their healthy alternatives. For example, if we know that the theme of your adversity is threat and you hold a rigid/extreme attitude towards that threat, we are well placed to conclude that you are experiencing anxiety. Similarly, if we know that the theme of your adversity is threat and you hold a flexible/non-extreme attitude towards that threat, we are well placed to conclude that you are experiencing concern. Table 1.1 puts this more succinctly.

Table 1.1 Inference themes, attitudes and emotions

Inference theme	Attitude	Emotion
Threat	Rigid/extreme	Anxiety
Threat	Flexible/non-extreme	Concern

Associated behaviour

So far, I have mentioned that one way of distinguishing between an emotional problem and its HNE alternative is to take the theme of what the person has feelings about with respect to the adversity they are facing and the attitude the person holds that accounts for the emotion. You have learned the following:

adversity inference theme + rigid/extreme attitude = emotional problem
adversity inference theme + flexible/non-extreme attitude = HNE

Now, when you hold an attitude towards an adversity, you don't just experience an emotion, you also experience a tendency to act in a certain way (known as an action tendency), which you may or may not convert into overt behaviour.

Thus, another way to tell if what you feel in a specific situation is an emotional problem or an HNE is to examine how you acted or, if you did not take action, to examine your action tendency. Let me illustrate this when a person is trying to figure out whether the anger that they felt was negative and unhealthy, or negative but healthy.

Geraldine was angry with her boss when he did not recommend her for promotion, an advancement that she considered she thoroughly deserved. Geraldine considered that her boss had acted in a very unfair manner towards her. Geraldine was unsure whether her anger was negative and unhealthy, or negative but healthy, so she considered how she acted in the situation. This did not help her because she did not take any action when she discovered the news, nor subsequently. Finally, she considered what she felt like doing, but did not do. Geraldine's action tendency was to scream abuse at her boss and to get revenge against him by getting him into trouble with his own boss. Such action tendencies were clearly hostile in nature and showed Geraldine that her anger was an emotional problem.

When you hold a rigid/extreme attitude towards an adversity, your behaviour (or action tendencies) will tend to be dysfunctional and will prevent you from dealing with the adversity in a constructive manner. Whereas, when you hold a flexible/non-extreme attitude towards an adversity, your behaviour (or action tendencies) will tend to be functional and will help you to deal with the adversity in a constructive manner.

Associated thinking

The final way of determining whether you are experiencing an emotional problem or an HNE about an adversity is to inspect the thinking that is associated with the emotion. This is different from the inference that you made about the situation that constituted your adversity. Such thinking has not yet been processed by your attitudes. The thinking that I am referring to here is the thinking that is associated with your emotion. This is the thinking that has been produced when your adversity has been processed by your attitudes. When your adversity has been processed by rigid/extreme attitudes, the thinking that results is very likely to be highly distorted and skewed to the negative in content and ruminative in nature. However, when this adversity has been processed by flexible/non-extreme attitudes, the thinking that results is very likely to be realistic and balanced in content and non-ruminative in nature. David Burns, a leading cognitive therapist, first outlined in his book *Feeling Good: The New Mood Therapy* (Burns, 1980) a list of thinking errors – which are by nature highly distorted and skewed to the negative – that people make when they process adversities with rigid/extreme attitudes. I outline and illustrate some of these thinking errors and their realistic and balanced alternatives in Appendix 1. You should consult this list if you are unsure whether the thinking you engage in when you are experiencing an emotion is realistic and balanced or highly distorted and skewed to the negative.

Let me illustrate all this with reference to another person who is trying to figure out whether the anger that she felt was negative and unhealthy or negative but healthy.

Francine (a co-worker of Geraldine) was also angry with her boss when he did not recommend her for promotion, an advancement that she considered she thoroughly deserved. Francine considered that her boss had acted in a very unfair manner towards her. Francine was unsure whether her anger was negative and unhealthy, or negative but healthy, so she considered how she thought in the situation. She thought about asserting herself with her boss after planning what to say. After she had done this, she made an appointment to see her boss and, in the days that followed until the meeting, she thought about the issue in passing, but did not ruminate on the issue. Given that Francine's thinking that went along with her anger was realistic and balanced and non-ruminative in nature, she considered that her anger was an HNE and not an emotional problem.

Let me summarise the points that I have made in this section and the previous one on behaviour and add it to the material that I presented on p. 15 (see Table 1.2).

In the chapters that follow, I employ a similar structure. First, I outline the major factors that need to be considered when understanding the emotional problem under focus. Second, I show you what steps you need to take to change each emotional problem to an appropriate HNE. Finally, I discuss what you need to do to make yourself less prone to whatever emotional problems you are particularly susceptible to. Throughout each chapter, I illustrate the major points whenever relevant.

Table 1.2 Summary

Adversity inference theme +	Rigid/extreme attitude =	Emotional problem + Unconstructive behaviour and action tendencies + Highly distorted thinking that is skewed to the negative and ruminative in nature
Adversity inference theme +	Flexible/non-extreme attitude =	Healthy negative emotion (HNE) + Constructive behaviour and action tendencies + Realistic and balanced thinking that is non-ruminative in nature

NOTES

1 Throughout this book, I will refer to events where you don't get what you want, or get what you don't want, as 'adversities'.
2 We do not have agreed terms for HNEs. Thus, it is important that you use the terms that are meaningful to you if they are different from the terms in this list.

2

Dealing with anxiety

In this chapter, I begin by presenting REBT's way of understanding anxiety and then address how to deal with this very common emotional problem.

UNDERSTANDING ANXIETY

In understanding anxiety, we need to know what we tend to make ourselves anxious about (i.e., its major inference theme), what attitudes we hold, how we act or tend to act, and how we think when we are anxious.

Major inference themes in anxiety

When you are anxious, you are facing or think you are facing a threat to some aspect of your personal domain (see pp. 13–14). There are different forms of anxiety, which I list in Table 2.1 together with the typical threats that feature in them.

Rigid/extreme attitudes

As I explained in Chapter 1, according to REBT, an inference of threat that you make does not account for your emotional problem of anxiety. It is possible for you to make the same inference and be healthily concerned, but not anxious. In order for you to feel anxious when you infer the presence of threat to your personal domain, you have to hold a rigid/extreme attitude. While the rigid attitude is at the core of anxiety, the extreme attitudes that are derived from the rigid attitude often distinguish between whether you are experiencing ego anxiety (where you devalue yourself) and non-ego anxiety (where you 'awfulise' or find the adversity unbearable). You may, of course, experience both ego anxiety and non-ego anxiety in a given situation.

DOI: 10.4324/9781003424307-2

Table 2.1 Different types of anxiety and their major inference themes

Type of anxiety	Typical threats
Social anxiety	◉ Acting poorly in a social setting (e.g., revealing that you are anxious; saying something stupid; not knowing what to say) ◉ Being judged negatively by people
Health anxiety	◉ Being uncertain that a symptom that you have is not malignant
Generalised anxiety	◉ A general sense that you do not know that you are safe ◉ A general sense that something may happen that will result in you losing self-control in some way ◉ Thinking that you may become anxious
Public speaking anxiety	◉ Performing poorly while the focus of the audience is on you (e.g., going blank; revealing that you are anxious) ◉ Being judged negatively by people
Test anxiety	◉ Doing poorly on the test ◉ Going blank
Panic	◉ Not knowing that you will regain self-control immediately in a situation where you have begun to lose it

Behaviour associated with anxiety

When you hold a rigid/extreme attitude towards a threat to your personal domain, you feel anxious and you will act or tend to act in a number of ways, the most common of which are as follows:

◉ You avoid the threat.

◉ You withdraw physically from the threat.

◉ You ward off the threat (e.g., by rituals or superstitious behaviour).

- You try to neutralise the threat (e.g., by being nice to people of whom you are afraid).

- You distract yourself from the threat by engaging in other activity.

- You keep checking on the current status of the threat, hoping to find that it has disappeared or become benign.

- You seek reassurance from others that the threat is benign.

- You seek support from others so that, if the threat happens, they will handle it or be there to rescue you.

- You overprepare in order to minimise the threat happening or so that you are prepared to meet it (NB it is the overpreparation that is the problem here).

- You tranquilise your feelings so that you don't think about the threat.

- You overcompensate for feeling vulnerable by seeking out an even greater threat to prove to yourself that you can cope.

You will see from the above list that the main purpose of most of these behaviours (and action tendencies) is to keep you safe from the threat. However, such safety-seeking behaviour is largely responsible for the main-tenance of anxiety since it prevents you either from facing up to the situ-ation in which you think that the threat exists and dealing with the threat if it does exist, or from seeing that your inference of threat is inaccurate.

Overcompensation is particularly worthy of comment. Some people are intolerant of the feeling of vulnerability or non-coping that they experi-ence when they are anxious. They seek safety from the threat of non-coping by proving to themselves in actuality that they can cope with a greater threat. This is like a competition high jumper electing to jump a much greater height than the one at which she has twice failed. This is still a safety-seeking measure because the person seeks safety from the smaller threat by proving to herself that she can cope with the bigger threat.

Thinking associated with anxiety

When you hold a rigid/extreme attitude towards a threat to your personal domain, you will feel anxious and think in a number of ways. Remember what I said in Chapter 1: the thinking that accompanies your anxiety is the result of your threat being processed by your rigid/extreme attitude and therefore it is likely to contain a number of thinking errors that I present in Appendix 1. There are two types of post-rigid/extreme-attitude thinking that are important for you to understand:

- threat-exaggerating thinking; and
- safety-seeking thinking.

It is important to note that in both types of post-rigid/extreme-attitude thinking, such thinking may be in words or in mental images.

Threat-exaggerating thinking

In the first type of post-rigid/extreme-attitude thinking that is associated with anxiety – which I have called *threat-exaggerating thinking* – you elaborate and magnify the threat and its consequences in your mind as shown below:

- You overestimate the probability of the threat occurring.
- You underestimate your ability to cope with the threat.
- You ruminate about the threat.
- You create an even more negative threat in your mind.
- You magnify the negative consequences of the threat and minimise its positive consequences.
- You have more task-irrelevant thoughts than with concern.

Safety-seeking thinking

The second type of post-rigid/extreme-attitude thinking that is associated with anxiety is the thinking version of behaviour that is designed to keep you safe in the moment. I call this form of thinking *safety-seeking thinking*. Here are some common examples:

- You withdraw mentally from the threat.
- You try to persuade yourself that the threat is not imminent and that you are 'imagining' it.

- You think in ways designed to reassure yourself that the threat is benign or, if not, that its consequences will be insignificant.

- You distract yourself from the threat, e.g., by focusing on mental scenes of safety and well-being.

- You overprepare mentally in order to minimise the threat happening or so that you are prepared to meet it (NB once again it is the overpreparation that is the problem here).

- You picture yourself dealing with the threat in a masterful way.

- You overcompensate for your feeling of vulnerability by picturing yourself dealing effectively with an even bigger threat.

In the final two forms of thinking, the person is seeking safety from the threat of non-coping by mentally creating images of masterful coping.

One important point to note about these two forms of post-rigid/extreme-attitude thinking is that they are quite different: in one you elaborate and magnify the threat and in the other you are thinking of ways to protect yourself against the threat. You can, and people often do, switch rapidly between these different forms of thinking. The more your safety-seeking thinking fails, the more you will mentally elaborate and magnify the threat, and the more you do the latter, the more you will try to search mentally for safety.

HOW TO DEAL WITH ANXIETY

If you are prone to anxiety, you tend to experience this emotional problem in a variety of different settings and in response to a variety of threats. Here is how to deal with anxiety so that you become less prone to it.

Step 1: Identify reasons why anxiety is a problem for you and why you want to change

While anxiety is generally regarded as an emotional problem, it is useful for you to spell out reasons why anxiety is a problem for you and why you want to change. I suggest that you keep a written list of these reasons and refer to it as needed as a reminder of why you are engaged in a self-help programme. I discuss the healthy alternative to anxiety in Step 4.

Step 2: Take responsibility for your anxiety

In REBT, we argue that people or things do not make you anxious; rather you create these feelings by the rigid/extreme attitudes that you hold towards such people and things. You may object that this involves you blaming yourself for creating your anxious feelings, but this objection is based on a misconception. It assumes that taking responsibility for creating your anxiety is synonymous with self-blame. In truth, responsibility means that you take ownership for the rigid/extreme attitudes that underpin your anxiety while accepting yourself unconditionally for doing so. Blame, on the other hand, means that you regard yourself as worthless (for example) for creating your anxiety.

Step 3: Identify the threats you tend to be anxious about

The best way of identifying which threats you are particularly vulnerable to is to ask yourself whether or not such threats are to your self-esteem.

Major threats to self-esteem

- The prospect of failure
- The prospect of being disapproved of
- The prospect of being rejected
- The prospect of losing status

Major threats that do not involve your self-esteem

- The prospect of losing self-control (although this threat may involve your self-esteem as well)
- Uncertainty that one is not safe from threat
- The prospect of experiencing discomfort
- The prospect of loss of order

⊚ The prospect of experiencing certain internal processes (e.g., unwanted thoughts, feelings, images and urges). Again, this threat may involve self-esteem as well

Use the above list to identify the themes that you find threatening.

Step 4: Identify the three components of your anxiety response and set goals with respect to each component

The next step is for you to list the three elements of your anxiety response in the face of each of the threats listed above.

Identify the three components of your anxiety response

I use the term 'anxiety response' to describe the three main components that make up this response. The three components of your anxiety response are the emotional, behavioural and thinking components.

Emotional component

The emotional component is, of course, anxiety.

Behavioural component

The behavioural component concerns overt behaviour or action tendencies. These will be largely safety-seeking in nature. Consult the list that I provided to help you identify your behaviour associated with each theme when you are anxious (see pp. 20–21).

Thinking component

The thinking component concerns theme-exaggerated thinking or safety-seeking thinking. These may be in words or in mental pictures. Consult the list that I provided to help you identify your thinking associated with each theme when you are anxious (see pp. 22–23).

Set goals with respect to each of the three components

You need to set goals so that you know what you are striving for when you deal effectively with anxiety. The three goals are emotional, behavioural and thinking goals.

Emotional goal

Your emotional goal is concern rather than anxiety (or whatever synonym you prefer to the term 'concern'). Concern is an HNE, which is an appropriate response to threat, but one that helps you to process what has happened to you and move on with your life rather than get stuck or bogged down.

Behavioural goal

Your behavioural goal should reflect actions that are based on concern about the threat rather than anxiety. The following are the most common behaviours associated with concern rather than anxiety. You may wish to compare these behaviours with those associated with anxiety that I presented on pp. 20–21.

- You face up to the threat without using any safety-seeking measures.
- You take constructive action to deal with the threat.
- You seek support from others to help you face up to the threat and then take constructive action by yourself rather than rely on them to handle it for you.
- You prepare to meet the threat but do not overprepare.

You will note that this list is much shorter than the list outlining the behaviours that are associated with anxiety. The reason is that, when you seek safety from threat, there are far more ways of doing so than when you face up to the threat.

Thinking goal

As well as setting behavioural goals related to the feeling of concern in the face of threat, it is important that you set thinking goals associated with this emotion. The following are the most common forms of thinking associated with concern rather than anxiety. Again, you may wish to compare these forms of thinking with those associated with anxiety that I presented on pp. 22–23.

- You are realistic about the probability of the threat occurring.
- You view the nature of the threat realistically.
- You realistically appraise your ability to cope with the threat.
- You think about what to do concerning dealing with the threat constructively rather than ruminate about the threat.
- You have more task-relevant thoughts than with anxiety.

As the above list shows, the dominant feature of thinking associated with concern is that it is realistic and coping focused. Thus, when you are concerned, but not anxious, you do not elaborate or magnify the threat, nor do you mentally seek safety from it. Please remember that such thinking may be in words or in mental pictures.

Step 5: Identify your general rigid/extreme attitudes and alternative general flexible/non-extreme attitudes

A general rigid/extreme attitude is an attitude that you hold across situations defined by the theme that you find threatening. It accounts for your anxiety response. Its flexible/non-extreme alternative, which will also be general in nature, will account for your concern response.

I suggest that you identify both sets of attitudes at this point for a number of reasons (as follows). Doing so will help you to:

- see quickly what the alternatives to your rigid/extreme attitudes are;
- see that you can achieve your goals by acquiring and developing your flexible/non-extreme attitudes; and
- get the most out of examining your attitudes later.

Identify your general rigid/extreme attitudes

When you identify a general rigid/extreme attitude, you take a common theme (e.g., criticism or loss of self-control) and add to this a general rigid attitude and the main extreme attitude that is derived from the rigid attitude. Note the following:

⊙ If you are particularly prone to self-esteem based anxiety, your main extreme attitude will be a self-devaluation attitude.

⊙ For anxiety that is non-self-esteem based, your main extreme attitude will either be an awfulising attitude or an unbearability attitude, and less frequently it may be an other-devaluation attitude or a life-devaluation attitude.

For example:

⊙ 'I must not be criticised and, if I am, it would prove that I am worthless' (a general self-esteem based rigid/extreme attitude).

⊙ 'I must not lose self-control and it would be awful if I do' (a general non-self-esteem based rigid/extreme attitude).

Identify your alternative general flexible/non-extreme attitudes

When you identify your alternative general flexible/non-extreme attitude, you take the same common theme (e.g., criticism or loss of self-control) and add to this a general flexible attitude and the main non-extreme attitude that is derived from the flexible attitude. Note the following:

⊙ If your general extreme attitude is self-devaluation (when you are particularly prone to self-esteem based anxiety), then your general non-extreme attitude will be an unconditional self-acceptance attitude.

⊙ If you are prone to non-self-esteem based anxiety, then your alternative general non-extreme attitude will be a non-awfulising attitude, a bearability attitude and less frequently an unconditional other-acceptance attitude or an unconditional life-acceptance attitude.

For example:

⊙ ('I would prefer not to be criticised, but I don't have to be immune to criticism.) If I am criticised, it would be unpleasant, but it would not prove that I am worthless. I am the same fallible human being whether I am criticised or not' (a general unconditional self-acceptance attitude).

⊚ ('I would much prefer not to lose self-control, but that doesn't mean that I must not do so.) If I do lose self-control, it would be very bad, but it would not be awful' (a general non-awfulising attitude).

Step 6: Examine your general attitudes

While there are many ways of examining your general rigid/extreme attitudes and general flexible/non-extreme attitudes, in my view the most efficient way involves you first examining together your general rigid attitude and its general flexible attitude alternative and then examining together your main general extreme attitude and your main general non-extreme attitude.

Examine your general rigid attitude and its general flexible attitude alternative

First, take your general rigid attitude and its general flexible attitude alternative and write them down next to one another on a sheet of paper. Then ask yourself:

⊚ Which is true and which is false?

⊚ Which is sensible logically and which does not make sense?

⊚ Which has largely constructive results and which has largely unconstructive results?

Write down your answer to each of these questions on your piece of paper, giving reasons for each answer. Consult Appendix 2 for help with the answers to these questions, which you need to adapt and apply to the attitudes you are examining.

Examine your main general extreme attitude and its general non-extreme attitude alternative

Next, take your main general extreme attitude and its general non-extreme attitude alternative and again write them down next to one another on a sheet of paper. Then, ask yourself the same three questions that you used with your general rigid attitude and its general flexible attitude alternative. Again, write down your answer to each of these questions on your piece of paper, giving reasons for each answer. I suggest that you consult Appendix 3 (for help with examining awfulising attitudes and non-awfulising attitudes), Appendix 4 (for help with examining unbearability attitudes and bearability attitudes) and Appendix 5 (for help with examining devaluation attitudes and unconditional acceptance attitudes). Again, you need to adapt and apply these arguments to the attitudes you are examining.

You should now be ready to commit to acting and thinking in ways consistent with your general flexible/non-extreme attitude. For, unless you do so, you will not strengthen your conviction in this attitude.

Step 7: Face your threat in imagery

I hope that you have made a commitment to act on your general flexible and relevant non-extreme attitudes. Assuming that you have, your basic task is to face up to your threat while not using any of the safety-seeking behavioural measures that you employed to keep yourself safe from the threat when you were anxious.

Up to this point, you have worked at a general level concerning the threats you are anxious about, the general rigid/extreme attitudes that account for this anxiety and their alternative general flexible/non-extreme attitudes. However, when you come to apply your general flexible/non-extreme attitudes in dealing with your threats, you need to consider one important point. Since you make yourself anxious about threats in specific situations (actual or imagined), you need to deal with these specific threats by rehearsing specific variants of your general flexible/non-extreme attitudes.

While the best way to do this is in specific situations where you infer threat, you may benefit from using imagery first. If this is the case, you need to do the following:

⦿ Imagine a specific situation in which you felt anxious or may feel anxious and focus on your threat.

⦿ See yourself facing the threat while rehearsing a specific flexible/non-extreme attitude relevant to the situation. As you do this, try to make yourself feel concerned, rather than anxious.

⦿ Then, see yourself take action without using the safety-seeking behavioural measures you would generally use if you were anxious. Make your picture realistic. Imagine yourself experiencing the urge to use your safety-seeking behaviours, but not doing so. Also, picture yourself acting functionally, but with a faltering performance rather than a masterful one.

- Recognise that some of your post-rigid/extreme-attitude thinking may be distorted. Respond to it without getting bogged down doing so. Accept the presence of any remaining distorted thoughts without engaging with them.

- Repeat the above steps until you feel sufficiently ready to put this sequence into practice in your life.

If you find that facing your threat, in your mind's eye, is too much for you, use a principle that I call 'challenging, but not overwhelming'. This means that, instead of imagining yourself facing a threat that you find 'overwhelming' at the present time, choose a similar threat to face that you would find 'challenging, but not overwhelming'. Then employ the same steps that I have outlined above. Work in this way with modified threats until you find your original threat 'challenging, but not overwhelming' and then use the steps again.

Step 8: Face your threat in reality

Whether or not you have used imagery as a preparatory step, you need to take the following steps when you face your threat in reality.

- Choose a specific situation in which the threat is likely to occur and about which you would ordinarily feel anxious.

- Make a plan of how you are going to deal with the threat and resolve not to use any of your behavioural, safety-seeking measures.

- Rehearse a specific version of your general flexible/non-extreme attitudes before entering the situation so that you can face your threat while in a healthy[1] frame of mind. In addition, it would be useful to develop a shorthand version of your specific flexible/non-extreme attitude to use while you are in the situation.

- Enter the situation and accept the fact that you are likely to be uncomfortable while doing so. Do not take any safety-seeking measures and take action as previously planned. React to any consequences from a healthy frame of mind if you can.

⊚ Recognise that, even though you have got yourself into a healthy frame of mind, some of your thinking may be distorted and unrealistic and some may be realistic and balanced. Accept the presence of the former and do not engage with it. Engage with the latter without using it to reassure yourself.

Step 9: Capitalise on what you have learned

When you have faced your threat and dealt with it as best you can, it is important that you reflect on what you did and what you learned. In particular, if you were able to face your threat, rehearse your specific flexible/non-extreme attitudes and take constructive action, then ask yourself how you can capitalise on what you achieved. If you experienced any problems, respond to the following questions:

⊚ Did I face the threat and, if not, why not?

⊚ Did I rehearse my flexible/non-extreme attitudes before and during facing the threat and, if not, why not?

⊚ Did I execute my plan to face the threat and, if not, why not?

⊚ Did I use safety-seeking measures and, if so, why?

⊚ Did I engage with post-rigid/extreme attitude distorted thinking and, if so, why?

Reflect on your experience and put into practice what you have learned the next time you face the threat.

Step 10: Generalise your learning

While you can only face and deal with a threat in specific situations, you can generalise what you have learned about dealing effectively with anxiety across situations defined by a threat to which you are particularly vulnerable (e.g., disapproval) and also apply your learning to situations defined by a different threat that you may have problems with (e.g., criticism).

Fiona was particularly prone to anxiety about being disapproved of, so she followed the steps outlined in this chapter. Thus:

- Fiona assessed the three components of her anxiety response and set goals with respect to all three components.

- She identified her relevant general rigid/extreme attitude towards disapproval (i.e., 'I must not be disapproved of. If I am, I am worthless') that underpinned her anxiety response and her alternative general flexible/non-extreme attitude (i.e., 'I don't want to receive disapproval, but that does not mean I must not be disapproved of. If I am, it's unfortunate, but it does not prove I'm worthless. I am a unique, unrateable, fallible human being whether I am approved or disapproved of') that underpinned her concern response.

- She examined both elements of her general rigid/extreme attitude and her flexible/non-extreme attitude until she clearly saw that the former were false, made no sense and were detrimental to her, and that the latter were true, sensible and healthy.

- She outlined situations where she particularly feared disapproval and prepared to face them by examining specific versions of these attitudes. She first rehearsed relevant specific versions of her general flexible/non-extreme attitude towards disapproval and faced her threat in these specific situations while keeping in mind a shortened version of her flexible/non-extreme attitude (i.e., 'I'm fallible, although disapproved of') and without using her behavioural and thinking safety-seeking measures regarding disapproval. As she did so, she tolerated the discomfort that she felt and accepted that some of her 'threat-elaborated' thinking would still be in her mind. She let such thinking be without engaging with it, suppressing it or distracting herself from it.

- When she had made progress in dealing with her disapproval anxiety, Fiona applied the common features to her fear of failure. She also identified new behavioural and thinking components of her anxiety response with respect to failure and set goals accordingly.

- She identified her relevant general rigid/extreme attitude towards regarding failure (i.e., 'I must not fail and, if I do, I am a failure') that underpinned her anxiety response and her alternative general flexible/non-extreme attitude (i.e., 'I don't want to fail, but I don't always have to succeed. It's bad if I fail, but that does not mean I am a failure. I am a unique, unrateable, fallible human being whether I succeed or fail') that underpinned her concern response.

- She again examined both elements of her general rigid/extreme attitude and her general flexible/non-extreme attitude until she clearly saw that the former was false, made no sense and was detrimental to her and that the latter was true, sensible and healthy.

- She then outlined situations that she had avoided because she particularly feared failure and prepared to face them by examining specific versions of these attitudes. She first rehearsed relevant specific versions of her general flexible/non-extreme attitude towards failure and faced her threat in these specific situations while keeping in mind a shortened version of this attitude (i.e., 'I don't have to succeed') and without using her behavioural and thinking safety-seeking measures regarding failure.

- As she did so she tolerated the discomfort that she felt and accepted that some of her 'threat-elaborated' thinking would still be in her mind. She again let such thinking be without engaging with it, suppressing it or distracting herself from it.

As this section shows, you can generalise what you learn about dealing with anxiety from situation to situation as defined by a specific threat and from there to situations defined by a different threat with which you have a problem. If you do this with all the threats to which you are vulnerable, you will take the toxicity out of the emotional problem of anxiety!

USING REBT'S ABCD FORM TO DEAL WITH SPECIFIC EXAMPLES OF YOUR ANXIETY

This chapter is mainly geared to help you deal with your anxiety in general terms. However, you can also use this material to address specific examples of your anxiety. I have developed a self-help form to provide the structure to assist you in this regard. It is called the ABCD form and it appears with instructions in Appendix 6.

OTHER IMPORTANT ISSUES IN DEALING WITH ANXIETY

In the above section, I outlined a 10-step programme to deal with anxiety. In this section, I discuss some other important issues that may be relevant to you in your work to become less prone to this emotional problem. If you want to, you can incorporate them as additional steps in the above step-by-step guide at points relevant to you.

Why you overestimate threat and how to deal with it

If you are particularly prone to anxiety, you will be particularly sensitive to seeing threat where others, who are not prone to anxiety, do not. So far in this chapter, I have helped you deal with anxiety in situations where you perceive threat. In this section, I help you to understand and deal with situations where you overestimate threat in the first place.

Why you overestimate threat

This is how you come to overestimate threat in your area of vulnerability. I will illustrate this with reference to one of Fiona's general rigid/extreme attitudes:

- You take the theme of your general rigid/extreme attitude: disapproval from the general rigid/extreme attitude:

  'I must not be disapproved of. If I am, I am worthless.'

- You construct a second general rigid/extreme attitude that features uncertainty about the original threat theme:

  'I must be certain that I won't be disapproved of. I can't bear such uncertainty.'

- You bring this second general rigid/extreme attitude to situations where it is possible that you may be disapproved of and you make a threat-related inference in the absence of certainty from the threat:

  'Since I don't have certainty that I won't be disapproved of, then I will be disapproved of.'

- You focus on this inference and bring a specific version of your original general rigid/extreme attitude to this inference. For example:

  Inference: *'My classmates will disapprove of me.'*

  Specific rigid/extreme attitude: *'My classmates must not disapprove of me. If they do, I am worthless.'*

How to deal with your overestimations of threat

To deal with your overestimations of threat, you need to take a number of steps, which I will illustrate again with reference to Fiona.

⊚ Construct general flexible/non-extreme alternatives, both to your original threat-focused general rigid/extreme attitude:

'I don't want to receive disapproval, but that does not mean I must not be disapproved of. If I am, it's unfortunate, but it does not prove I'm worthless. I am a unique, unrateable, fallible human being whether I am approved or disapproved of.'

and to your second uncertainty-focused general rigid/extreme attitude:

'I would like to be certain that I won't be disapproved of, but I don't need such certainty. It is difficult not having this uncertainty, but I can bear not having it and it is worth bearing.'

⊚ Examine both sets of attitudes until you can see why the two general flexible/non-extreme attitudes are true, logical and healthy, and the two general rigid/extreme attitudes are false, illogical and unhealthy, and you can commit to implementing the former.

⊚ Bring your uncertainty-focused general flexible/non-extreme attitude to situations where it is possible that you may be disapproved of and make an inference based on the data at hand:

'I am not certain if I will be approved or disapproved of, so let's consider the evidence.'

⊚ If there is evidence indicating there is a good chance that you will be disapproved of, use a specific version of your general disapproval-focused flexible/non-extreme attitude to deal with this. For example:

Inference: *'My classmates will disapprove of me.'*

Specific flexible/non-extreme attitude: *'I don't want my classmates to disapprove of me, but they don't have to do what I want. If they do disapprove of me, that is uncomfortable, but I am not worthless. I am the same unique, unrateable person whether they approve or disapprove of me.'*

How to examine the accuracy of your inference of threat, if necessary

If you are still unsure if your inference of threat is accurate or inaccurate, answer one or more of the following questions:

- How likely is it that the threat happened (or might happen)?

- Would an objective jury agree that the threat actually happened or might happen? If not, what would the jury's verdict be?

- Did I view (am I viewing) the threat realistically? If not, how could I have viewed (can I view) it more realistically?

- If I asked someone whom I could trust to give me an objective opinion about the truth or falsity of my inference about the threat, what would the person say to me and why? How would this person encourage me to view the threat instead?

- If a friend had told me that they had faced (were facing or were about to face) the same situation as I faced and had made the same inference of threat, what would I say to them about the validity of their inference and why? How would I encourage the person to view the threat instead?

Assessing and dealing with emotional problems about anxiety

While there is quite a lot of evidence that animals get anxious in the presence of threat, there is little evidence that they make themselves disturbed about their anxiety. However, we humans do disturb ourselves about our anxiety and our other emotional problems. The technical term for this is meta-disturbance (literally disturbance about disturbance) and I will be discussing this phenomenon and how to deal with it here and in the following chapters. It is important to assess carefully the nature of this meta-disturbance before you can best deal with it.

The best way to start dealing with the assessment of any emotional problems you might have about anxiety is to ask yourself the question: 'How do I feel about being anxious?' The most common emotional problems that people have about anxiety are as follows: anxiety, depression, unhealthy regret, shame and unhealthy self-anger. I will discuss only the first of these in this chapter, i.e., anxiety about anxiety, and refer you to the respective chapters on depression, unhealthy regret, shame and unhealthy anger for help on how to deal with these meta-emotional problems (i.e., emotional problems about emotional problems) as applied to anxiety.

Assessing anxiety about anxiety

When you are anxious about anxiety, it is clear that you think of your original anxiety as some kind of threat. The most common of these threats are the following:

⊚ Anxiety is emotionally painful.

⊚ Anxiety means I am losing self-control.

⊚ Anxiety is a personal weakness.

Dealing with anxiety about anxiety

Unless you deal with your anxiety about anxiety (called meta-anxiety), you are unlikely to deal with your original anxiety, since your meta-anxiety will lead to general avoidance of situations in which you are likely to feel anxious. Since dealing with anxiety depends on you facing and not avoiding threat, meta-anxiety (if you experience it) often has to be dealt with before you deal with your original anxiety.

As I have made clear in this book, it is important that you develop flexible/non-extreme attitudes towards threat and face up to and deal constructively with it without making use of safety-seeking measures (both behavioural and thinking) and while letting be (i.e., not engaging with or distracting yourself from) any remaining threat-elaborating thoughts or images that you may have. With these points in mind, let me give you brief advice concerning how to deal with the three forms of anxiety about anxiety I have listed.

Dealing with the threat of the emotional pain of anxiety

First, commit yourself to going forward with the set of flexible/non-extreme attitudes towards the pain of anxiety after examining both your rigid/extreme and flexible/non-extreme attitudes as outlined in Appendices 2–4. These are likely to be non-ego in nature (e.g., 'I would prefer not to experience the emotional pain of anxiety, but I don't have to be immune to it. It's hard bearing such pain, but I can do so and it's worth doing so because it will help me deal with my original anxiety'). Then, develop a shorthand version of this flexible/non-extreme attitude (e.g., 'The pain of anxiety is bearable and worth bearing') and use this as you seek out situations in which you are likely to feel anxious, employing the 'challenging, but not overwhelming' principle described earlier (see p. 33). Do this without using safety-seeking measures until you are concerned about the pain of anxiety, but not anxious about it.

When you have done all this, you will probably see that anxiety may not be as emotionally painful as you previously thought.

Dealing with the threat of losing self-control when you are anxious

When you are anxious, you do begin to lose control of your feelings, sensations and thoughts. It is important for you to assess which aspect of loss of self-control you are anxious about. Then do the following. First, commit yourself to going forward with the set of flexible/non-extreme attitudes towards beginning to lose self-control (after examining both your rigid/extreme and flexible/non-extreme attitudes as outlined in Appendices 2–4). These are likely to be non-ego in nature (e.g., 'I would prefer not to lose control, but I don't always have to have such self-control and I don't have to regain it immediately when I have begun to lose it. It's unfortunate when I begin to lose self-control, but it isn't terrible'). Then, develop a shorthand version of this flexible/non-extreme attitude (e.g., 'I don't have to be in control') and use this as you seek out situations in which you are likely to feel anxious and begin to lose self-control. Again, employ the 'challenging, but not overwhelming' principle described earlier (see p. 33) and do so without using safety-seeking measures until you are concerned about losing self-control but not anxious about it. In particular, accept that you may have thoughts and images where you have lost complete control of yourself. These thoughts do not predict the future, but are the remnants of post-rigid/extreme-attitude thinking and need to be understood and accepted as such. Therefore, don't engage with them or distract yourself from them.

When you have taken these steps, you will probably realise that you have more self-control when you are anxious than you previously thought and that loss of complete self-control, while not impossible, is highly unlikely.

Dealing with the threat of anxiety being a personal weakness

The first step to dealing with this anxiety is to assume temporarily that anxiety is a personal weakness. First, commit yourself to going forward with the set of flexible/non-extreme attitudes towards having such a personal weakness (after examining both your rigid/extreme and flexible/

non-extreme attitudes as outlined in Appendices 2 and 5). These are likely to be ego in nature (e.g., 'I would prefer not to have this personal weakness, but that does not mean that I must not have it. I am not a weak person for having this unfortunate weakness. Rather, I am a fallible human being who has both strengths and weaknesses'). Then, develop a shorthand version of this flexible/non-extreme attitude (e.g., 'Anxiety means I'm fallible') and use this as you seek out situations in which you are likely to feel anxious, employing the 'challenging, but not overwhelming' principle described earlier (see p. 33). Do this, once again, without using safety-seeking measures until you are concerned about your 'personal weakness', but not anxious about it.

When you have done all this, you will probably see that anxiety may not be as much a personal weakness as you previously thought. To help consolidate this, ask yourself if you would tell a loved one that anxiety is a personal weakness.

Developing and rehearsing non-anxious, concern-based world views

People develop views of the world as it relates to them that make it more or less likely that they will experience unhealthy negative emotions (UNEs). The world views that render you vulnerable to anxiety do so in a similar way to your uncertainty-focused general rigid/extreme attitudes towards a specific threat theme by making you oversensitive to the presence of threat about which you hold anxiety-related rigid/extreme attitudes. However, these anxiety-based world views have this effect on you much more widely.

It is important that you develop realistic views of the world that will help you to deal with anxiety and experience healthy concern instead. In Table 2.2, you will find an illustrative list of such world views rather than an exhaustive one, so you can get an idea of what I mean. This will enable you to develop your own. In Table 2.2, I first describe a world view that renders you vulnerable to anxiety and then I give its healthy alternative. You will see that the latter views are characterised by complexity and being non-extreme in nature, whereas, in the former, aspects of the world that relate to threat are portrayed as unidimensional and extreme.

If you hold flexible/non-extreme attitudes that are consistent with the views of the world listed on the right-hand side of Table 2.2, and if you act and think in ways that are, in turn, consistent with these flexible/non-extreme attitudes, you will become less prone to anxiety.

Table 2.2 World views that render you vulnerable to anxiety and help you to deal with anxiety

Views of the world that render you vulnerable to anxiety	Views of the world that help you deal with anxiety
⦿ The world is a dangerous place	⦿ The world is a place where danger exists, but where there is much safety
⦿ Uncertainty is dangerous. Knowing in all probability that I am safe is not good enough	⦿ Uncertainty can indicate the presence of threat, but more often than not it is associated with the absence of threat, a sign that I am safe from threat. Probability of safety is all I have and is good enough for me
⦿ Not being in control is dangerous. Either I am in control or I am out of control	⦿ Not being in control is unpleasant, but is rarely dangerous. Just because I am not in complete control certainly does not mean that I am out of control
⦿ People cannot be trusted	⦿ People vary enormously along a continuum of trustworthiness. My best stance is to trust someone unless I have evidence to the contrary. If I am let down that is very unfortunate, but hardly terrible and won't unduly affect my stance towards the next person I meet

In Chapter 3, I discuss the equally common emotional problem of depression and how to deal with it.

NOTE

1 By 'healthy' here I mean flexible/non-extreme.

Dealing with depression

In this chapter, I begin by presenting REBT's way of understanding depression[1] and then address how to deal with this very common emotional problem.

UNDERSTANDING DEPRESSION

In understanding depression, we need to know what we tend to make ourselves depressed about (i.e., its major inference themes), what attitudes we hold, how we act or tend to act, and how we think when we are depressed.

The three realms of your personal domain that are implicated in depression

The three realms of your personal domain that are implicated in your depression are the autonomous, sociotropic and deservingness realms.

The autonomous realm

Here you value such things as freedom from influence, freedom from constraint, freedom to determine your fate, your independence, self-control and effective functioning.

The sociotropic realm

Here you value such things as your relationships with people, your connection to them, being loved, being approved, being cared for by them, being able to rely on them and also being able to look after them.

The deservingness realm

Here you value yourself and others being treated fairly by the world.

DOI: 10.4324/9781003424307-3

Major inference themes in depression

When you are depressed:

- You have experienced a loss from the sociotropic and/or autonomous realms of your personal domain.
- You have experienced a failure within the sociotropic and/or autonomous realms of your personal domain.
- You or others have experienced an undeserved plight.[2]

Rigid/extreme attitudes

As I explained in Chapter 1, according to REBT, inferences on their own do not account for emotional problems. It is possible, therefore, for you to make the same inferences as listed above and be sad but not depressed. For you to feel depressed when you infer the presence of loss, failure or undeserved plight, you have to hold a rigid and one or more extreme attitudes. While the rigid attitude is at the core of depression, the extreme attitudes that are derived from the rigid attitude often distinguish between whether you are experiencing ego depression (where you devalue yourself) or non-ego depression (where you 'awfulise' or find the adversity unbearable). You may, of course, experience both ego depression and non-ego depression in a given situation.

Behaviour associated with depression

When you hold a rigid/extreme attitude towards a loss, failure or undeserved plight within the relevant realm of your personal domain, you will feel depressed and then act or tend to act in a number of ways, the most common of which are as follows:

- You withdraw from reinforcements.
- You withdraw into yourself (particularly in autonomous depression).
- You become overly dependent on and seek to cling to others (particularly in sociotropic depression).

- You bemoan your fate or that of others to anyone who will listen (particularly in plight-based depression – also called pity-based depression, see below).

- You create an environment consistent with your depressed feelings.

- You attempt to terminate feelings of depression in self-destructive ways.

You will see from the above list that these behaviours get in the way of you processing your loss, failure or undeserved plight so that you can grieve appropriately, integrate it into your attitude system and move on with pursuing your life's goals.

Thinking associated with depression

When you hold a rigid/extreme attitude towards a loss, failure or undeserved plight, you will feel depressed and then think in a number of ways. Remember what I said in Chapter 1: the thinking that accompanies your depression is the result of your loss, failure or undeserved plight being processed by your rigid/extreme attitude, and therefore it is likely to contain a number of thinking errors that I present in Appendix 1. I list the main features of this post-rigid/extreme-attitude thinking below:

- You see only negative aspects of the loss, failure or undeserved plight.

- You think of other losses, failures and undeserved plights that you (and, in the case of the latter, others) have experienced.

- You think you are unable to help yourself (helplessness).

- You see only pain and blackness in the future (hopelessness).

- You see yourself being totally dependent on others (in autonomous depression).

- You see yourself as being disconnected from others (in sociotropic depression).

- You see the world as full of undeservedness and unfairness (in plight-based depression).

- You tend to ruminate concerning the source of your depression and its consequences.

As you can see, such thinking exaggerates the negativity of loss, failure and undeserved plight and the consequences of each. As with post-rigid/extreme attitude anxiety thinking, post-rigid/extreme-attitude thinking may be in words or in mental images.

HOW TO DEAL WITH DEPRESSION

If you are prone to depression, you tend to experience this emotional problem in a variety of different settings and in response to a variety of losses, failures and undeserved plights. Here is how to deal with depression so that you become less prone to it.

Step 1: Identify reasons why depression is a problem for you and why you want to change

While depression is generally regarded as an emotional problem, it is useful for you to spell out reasons why depression is a problem for you and why you want to change. I suggest that you keep a written list of these reasons and refer to it as needed as a reminder of why you are engaged in a self-help programme. I discuss the healthy alternative to depression in Step 5.

Step 2: Become active

Before you focus on the psychological work that you will need to do to deal effectively with your depression, you need to become active. As I pointed out earlier in this chapter, when you are depressed you tend to become inactive quite quickly and, if you allow this to continue, such inactivity leads to more negative thinking, which, in turn, leads to decreased activity.

Therefore, the sooner you can go against your tendency to be inactive the better. If your inactivity has not become ingrained, increased activity will help you in two ways. First, such activity can be an antidepressant, particularly if it involves taking exercise. Indeed, running has been shown to be an effective way to deal with mild depression. Second, increased activity enables you to concentrate better on the psychological work that the remaining steps that I will discuss call for.

However, what can you do if you have become very inactive and just don't think that you can become more active or, if you did, that it wouldn't make any difference? You need to see such resistance to becoming active as depressed thinking, which stems from the rigid/extreme attitudes that led to your depression in the first place. Rather than respond to it, it is important that you test these thoughts out behaviourally. Thus, if you think that you can't become active, test it out by seeing if you can walk to the end of the road. If you can do that, then take another step and proceed, bit by bit, until you have become more active. At that point, you can judge whether or not becoming more active has had any impact on your mood. A pound to a penny it has.

When you have improved your mood to the point that you can concentrate, then you are ready to take responsibility for your depression in Step 3.

Step 3: Take responsibility for your depression

In REBT, we argue that people or things do not make you depressed; rather you create these feelings by the rigid/extreme attitudes that you hold towards such people and things. You may object that this involves you blaming yourself for creating your depressed feelings, but this objection is based on a misconception. It assumes that taking responsibility for creating your depression is synonymous with self-blame. In truth, responsibility means that you take ownership for the rigid/extreme attitudes that underpin your depression while accepting yourself unconditionally for doing so. Blame, on the other hand, means that you regard yourself as being bad or worthless for creating your depression.

Step 4: Identify the themes you tend to be depressed about

The best way of identifying depression-related inference themes to which you are particularly vulnerable is by understanding the themes associated with sociotropic depression, autonomous depression and plight-based or pity-based depression, and seeing which are present when you feel depressed.

Common themes in sociotropic depression

Themes in sociotropic depression include the following:

- disapproval

- rejection
- criticism
- loss of love
- negative evaluation from others
- losing connection with significant others
- being on one's own
- loss of reputation or social standing
- not being looked after or cared for
- not having anyone to look after or care for.

Common themes in autonomous depression

Themes in autonomous depression include the following:

- failure
- goals blocked
- loss of status
- loss of autonomy
- inability to do prized activities (e.g., because of sudden disability)
- being dependent on others
- loss of choice
- loss of self-control
- freedom curtailed.

The theme in pity-based depression

An undeserved plight has (or you think that it has) happened to you or to others. Here are some examples:

- You may have been made redundant by a company after working very hard for it for many years.
- A major catastrophe happens to people already struggling with their lives.

Step 5: Identify the three components of your depression response and set goals with respect to each component

The next step is for you to list the three elements of your depression response in the face of each of the threats listed above.

Identify the three components of your depression response

I use the term 'depression response' to describe the three main components that make up this response. The three components of your depression response are the emotional, behavioural and thinking components.

Emotional component

The emotional component here is, of course, depression.

Behavioural component

The behavioural component concerns overt behaviour or action tendencies. These will largely reflect your withdrawal from key aspects of life. Consult the list I provided to help you identify your behaviour associated with each theme when you are depressed (see pp. 43–44).

Thinking component

The thinking component associated with depression concerns magnification of the negative features of the situation you are in and its future implications. These may be in words or in mental pictures. Consult the list that I provided to help you identify your thinking associated with each theme when you are depressed (see p. 44).

Set goals with respect to each of the three components

You need to set goals so that you know what you are striving for when you deal effectively with depression. The three goals are emotional, behavioural and thinking goals.

Emotional goal

Your emotional goal is sadness rather than depression (or whatever synonym you prefer to the term 'sadness'). Sadness is an HNE, which is an appropriate response to loss, failure or undeserved plight, but one that helps you to process what has happened to you (or others in the case of undeserved plight) and move on with your life rather than get stuck or bogged down.

Behavioural goal

Your behavioural goal should reflect actions that are based on sadness about your inferential theme rather than depression. The following are the most common behaviours associated with sadness. You may wish to compare these behaviours with those associated with depression that I presented on pp. 43–44.

⊙ You seek out reinforcements after a period of mourning (particularly when your inferential theme is loss).

⊙ You create an environment inconsistent with depressed feelings.

⊙ You express your feelings about the loss, failure or undeserved plight, and talk in a non-complaining way about your feelings to significant others.

Thinking goal

As well as setting behavioural goals related to the feeling of sadness in the face of loss, failure and undeserved plight, it is important that you set thinking goals associated with this emotion. The following are the most common forms of thinking associated with sadness rather than depression. Again, you may wish to compare these forms of thinking with those associated with depression that I presented on p. 44.

⊙ You are able to recognise both negative and positive aspects of the loss or failure.

⊙ You think you are able to help yourself.

⊙ You look to the future with hope.

As the above list shows, the dominant feature of thinking associated with sadness is that it is realistic and optimistic. Please remember that such thinking may be in words or in mental pictures.

Step 6: Identify your general rigid/extreme attitudes and alternative general flexible/non-extreme attitudes

A general rigid/extreme attitude leading to your depression response is an attitude that you hold across situations defined by a loss theme, a failure theme or an undeserved plight theme. Its flexible/non-extreme attitude alternative, which will also be general in nature, will account for your sadness response.

Identify your general rigid/extreme attitudes

When you identify a general rigid/extreme attitude, you take a common theme (e.g., rejection, loss of autonomy or unfair suffering) and add to this a general rigid attitude and the main extreme attitude that is derived from the rigid attitude. When you are particularly prone to self-esteem based depression, then your main extreme attitude will be a self-devaluation attitude. For non-self-esteem based depression, your main extreme attitude may be either an awfulising attitude or an unbearability attitude, and less frequently it may be an other-devaluation attitude or a life-devaluation attitude. For example:

- 'I must not be rejected and, if I am, it would prove that I am unlovable' (a general self-esteem based rigid/extreme attitude).

- 'I must not be dependent on others and it would be awful if I were' (a general non-self-esteem based rigid/extreme attitude).

Identify your alternative general flexible/non-extreme attitudes

When you identify your alternative general flexible/non-extreme attitude, you take the same common theme (e.g., rejection, loss of autonomy or unfair suffering) and add to this a general flexible attitude and the main non-extreme attitude that is derived from the flexible attitude. If your general extreme attitude is self-devaluation (when you are particularly prone to self-esteem based depression), your general non-extreme attitude will be an unconditional self-acceptance attitude. If you are prone to non-self-esteem based depression, your alternative general non-extreme attitudes will be a non-awfulising attitude, a bearability attitude and less frequently an unconditional other-acceptance attitude or an unconditional life-acceptance attitude. For example:

⦿ 'I would prefer not to be rejected, but I don't have to be immune to rejection. If I am rejected, it would be painful, but it would not prove that I am unlovable. I am the same person whether I am rejected or accepted' (a general flexible/unconditional self-acceptance based attitude).

⦿ 'I would much prefer not to be dependent on others, but that doesn't mean that I must not be so. If I do have to be dependent on others, it would be very bad, but it would not be awful' (a general flexible/non-awfulising based attitude).

Step 7: Examine your general attitudes

I recommended in Chapter 2 that you first examine together your general rigid attitude and your alternative general flexible attitude and then examine together your main general extreme attitude and your alternative main general non-extreme attitude.

Examine your general rigid attitude and its general flexible attitude alternative

First, take your general rigid attitude and its general flexible attitude alternative and write them down next to one another on a sheet of paper. Then ask yourself:

⦿ Which is true and which is false?

⦿ Which is sensible logically and which does not make sense?

⦿ Which has largely constructive results and which has largely unconstructive results?

Write down your answer to each of these questions on your piece of paper, giving reasons for each answer. Consult Appendix 2 for help with the answers to these questions, which you need to adapt and apply to the attitudes you are examining.

Examine your general extreme attitude and its general non-extreme attitude alternative

Next, take your main general extreme attitude and its general non-extreme attitude alternative and again write them down next to one another on a sheet of paper. Then, ask yourself the same three questions that you used with your general rigid attitude and its general flexible attitude alternative. Again, write down your answer to each of these questions on your piece of paper, giving reasons for each answer. I suggest that you consult Appendix 3 (for help with examining awfulising attitude and non-awfulising attitudes), Appendix 4 (for help with examining unbearability attitudes and bearability attitudes) and Appendix 5 (for help with examining devaluation attitudes and unconditional acceptance attitudes). Again, you need to adapt and apply these arguments to the attitudes you are examining.

You should now be ready to commit to act and think in ways consistent with your general flexible/non-extreme attitude.

Step 8: Face your loss, failure and undeserved plight in imagery

I hope that you have made a commitment to act on your general flexible/ non-extreme attitude. Assuming that you have, your basic task is for you to face up to your loss, failure or undeserved plight and to learn to think in a flexible/non-extreme way about it without withdrawing from life.

Up to this point you have worked at a general level with respect to the losses, failures or undeserved plights you are depressed about, the general rigid/extreme attitudes that account for this depression and their alternative general flexible/non-extreme attitudes. However, when you come to apply your general flexible/non-extreme attitudes in dealing with your loss, failure or undeserved plight, you need to bear in mind one important point. Since you make yourself depressed about specific losses, failures or undeserved plights (actual or imagined), you need to deal with these specific losses by rehearsing specific variants of your general flexible/non-extreme attitudes.

While the best way to do this is in specific situations in which you infer loss, failure or undeserved plight, you may derive benefit by using imagery first. If this is the case, you need to do the following:

- Imagine a specific situation in which you felt depressed or may feel depressed and focus on your loss, failure or undeserved plight.

- See yourself facing the loss, failure or undeserved plight while rehearsing a specific flexible/non-extreme attitude relevant to the situation. As you do this, try to make yourself feel sad, rather than depressed.

- Then see yourself getting on with your life after an appropriate period of mourning. As you picture yourself getting on with your life, recognise that it is healthy to feel sad, even well after the event. The main thing is that your sadness does not stop you from reconnecting with life and pursuing your goals.

- Recognise that some of your post-rigid/extreme-attitude thinking may be distorted. Respond to it without getting bogged down doing so. Accept the presence of any remaining distorted thoughts without engaging with them.

- Repeat the above steps until you feel sufficiently ready to put this sequence into practice in your life.

If you find that facing your loss, failure or undeserved plight, in your mind's eye, is too much for you, use the 'challenging, but not overwhelming' principle that I introduced in Chapter 2 (see p. 33). This means that, instead of imagining yourself facing a loss, failure or undeserved plight that you find 'overwhelming' at the present time, choose a similar loss, failure or undeserved plight that you would find 'challenging, but not overwhelming'. Then employ the same steps that I have outlined above. Work in this way with modified losses, failures or undeserved plights until you find your original one 'challenging, but not overwhelming' and then use the steps again.

Step 9: Face your loss, failure and undeserved plight in reality

Whether or not you have used imagery as a preparatory step, you need to take the following steps when you face situations that remind you of your loss, failure or undeserved plight in reality.

- Choose a specific situation in which you will be reminded of your loss, failure or undeserved plight and about which you would ordinarily feel depressed.

- Rehearse a specific version of your general flexible/non-extreme attitude before entering the situation so that you can face your loss, failure or underserved plight while in a flexible/non-extreme frame of mind. In addition, it would be useful to develop a shorthand version of your specific flexible/non-extreme attitude to use while you are in the situation.

- Enter the situation and accept the fact that you are likely to be uncomfortable while doing so. React to any consequences from a flexible/non-extreme frame of mind if you can.

- Recognise that, even though you have got yourself into a flexible/non-extreme frame of mind, some of your thinking may be distorted and unrealistic and some may be realistic and balanced. Accept the presence of the former and do not engage with it. Engage with the latter without using it to reassure yourself.

Step 10: Capitalise on what you have learned

When you have faced the situation that reminded you of your loss, failure or undeserved plight and dealt with it as best you could, it is important that you reflect on what you did and what you learned. In particular, if you were able to face the situation, and rehearse your specific flexible/non-extreme attitudes until you felt sad, then ask yourself how you can capitalise on what you achieved. If you experienced any problems, respond to the following questions:

- Did I face the situation and, if not, why not?

- Did I rehearse my flexible/non-extreme attitudes before and during facing the situation and, if not, why not?

- Did I execute my plan to face the situation and, if not, why not?

- Did I engage with post-rigid/extreme attitude distorted thinking and, if so, why?

Reflect on your experience and put into practice what you have learned the next time you face a situation that reminds you of your loss, failure or undeserved plight.

Step 11: Generalise your learning

Once you have dealt with your depression in a specific situation, you can generalise what you have learned about dealing effectively with depression across situations defined by a loss, failure or undeserved plight to which you are particularly vulnerable to (e.g., failure) and also apply your learning to situations defined by a different theme that you may have problems with (e.g., having to rely on others).

James was particularly prone to depression about failure, so he followed the steps outlined in this chapter. Thus:

⦿ James assessed the three components of his depression response and set goals with respect to all three components.

⦿ He identified his relevant general rigid/extreme attitude regarding failure (i.e., 'I must not fail and, if I do, I'm a failure') that underpinned his depression response and his alternative general flexible/non-extreme attitude (i.e., 'I don't want to fail, but I am not immune to doing so and nor do I have to have such immunity. If I do fail it is bad, but I am not a failure. I am a unique, unrateable, fallible human being capable of failing and succeeding') that underpinned his sadness response.

⦿ He examined both elements of his general rigid/extreme attitude and his general flexible/non-extreme attitude until he clearly saw that the former were false, made no sense and were detrimental to him, and that the latter were true, sensible and healthy.

⦿ He outlined situations that particularly reminded him of his failures and prepared to face them by examining specific versions of these attitudes. He first rehearsed relevant specific versions of his general flexible/non-extreme attitudes regarding failure and then faced specific situations that reminded him of failing while keeping in mind a shortened version of his flexible/non-extreme attitude (i.e., 'I don't have to succeed'). As he did so, he tolerated the discomfort that he felt and accepted that some of his distorted and skewed negative thinking would still be in his mind. He let such thinking be without engaging with it, suppressing it or distracting himself from it.

⦿ When he had made progress in dealing with his failure-related depression, he applied common features to his depression about being dependent on others. He also identified new behavioural and thinking components of his depression response with respect to being dependent on others and set goals accordingly.

- He identified his relevant general rigid/extreme attitude regarding being dependent on others (i.e., 'I must not be dependent on others and, if I am, I am a pathetic individual') that underpinned his depression response and his alternative general flexible/non-extreme attitude (i.e., 'I don't want to be dependent on others, but that does not mean that this must not happen. If it does, it is really unpleasant, but it does not prove that I am a pathetic individual. It means that I am a fallible, ordinary person and my temporary dependent state does not define me') that underpinned his sadness response.

- He again examined both elements of his general rigid/extreme attitude and his general flexible/non-extreme attitude until he clearly saw that the former were false, made no sense and were detrimental to him, and that the latter were true, sensible and healthy.

- He then outlined situations that he had avoided because he would be dependent on others and would depress himself about that and prepared to face them by examining specific versions of these attitudes. He first rehearsed relevant specific versions of his general flexible/non-extreme attitude regarding being dependent and faced specific situations in which he would be dependent on others while keeping in mind a shortened version of his flexible/non-extreme attitude (i.e., 'Being dependent does not taint me').

- As he did so, he tolerated the discomfort that he felt and accepted that some of his distorted and skewed negative thinking would still be in his mind. He again let such thinking be without engaging with it, suppressing it or distracting himself from it.

As this section shows, you can generalise what you learn about dealing with depression from situation to situation as defined by a specific loss, failure or undeserved plight and from there to situations defined by a different theme related to depression with which you have a problem. If you do this with all losses, failures and undeserved plights to which you are particularly vulnerable, you will take the toxicity out of the emotional problem of depression!

USING REBT'S ABCD FORM TO DEAL WITH SPECIFIC EXAMPLES OF YOUR DEPRESSION

This chapter is mainly geared to help you deal with your depression in general terms. However, you can also use this material to address specific examples of your depression. I have developed a self-help form to provide the structure to assist you in this regard. It is called the ABCD form and it appears with instructions in Appendix 6.

OTHER IMPORTANT ISSUES IN DEALING WITH DEPRESSION

In the above section, I outlined an 11-step programme to deal with depression. In this section, I discuss some other important issues that may be relevant to you in your work to become less prone to this emotional problem. If you want to, you can incorporate them as additional steps in the above step-by-step guide at points relevant to you.

Why you focus so much on loss, failure and undeserved plight and how to deal with this

If you are particularly prone to depression, you will be particularly sensitive to focusing on the losses, failures and undeserved plights of your life (and in the lives of others in the case of the latter). You may see losses without seeing gains, you may see failures in what others regard as successes and you may fail to see the good in your life and in the lives of others. So far in this chapter, I have helped you deal with depression in situations where you perceive loss, failure and undeserved plight. In this section, I help you to understand and deal with situations where you overly focus on loss, failure or undeserved plight in the first place.

Why you focus so much on loss, failure and undeserved plight

The following explains why you focus so much on loss, failure and undeserved plight. I will illustrate this with reference to one of James' general rigid/extreme attitudes:

⊚ You take your general rigid/extreme attitude:

   'I must do perfectly well and, if I do not, I'm a failure.'

- You add the concept of uncertainty to this attitude so that you create a second general rigid/extreme attitude that features this uncertainty:

  'I must be sure that I have done perfectly well and I can't bear not knowing this.'

- You bring this second general rigid/extreme attitude to situations where you have not done perfectly well and make an inference coloured by this second general rigid/extreme attitude:

  'Since I don't know that I have done perfectly well, I have failed.'

- You focus on this inference and bring a specific version of your original general rigid/extreme attitude to this inference. For example:

  Inference: *'I got 90 per cent on that test. As I could have done better, I have failed.'*

  Specific rigid/extreme attitude: *'I absolutely should not have failed on the test. I am a failure for not doing better.'*

How to deal with your selective focus on loss, failure and undeserved plight

In order to deal with your selective focus on loss, failure or undeserved plight, you need to take a number of steps, which I illustrate with reference to James.

- Construct general flexible/non-extreme alternatives, both to your original loss-based, failure-based or undeserved plight-based rigid/extreme attitude:

  'I want to do perfectly well, but I don't have to do so. If I don't do perfectly well, it is bad, but I am not a failure. I am a unique, unrateable, fallible human being capable of failing and succeeding.'

and to your second general rigid/extreme attitude towards uncertainty related to your performance:

  'I would like to be sure that I have done perfectly well, but I really don't have to know this. If I don't, it is hard to bear, but I can bear such uncertainty and it's worth it for me to do so.'

- Examine both sets of attitudes until you can see the truth, logic and healthiness of the two general flexible/non-extreme attitudes and the falseness, illogicality and detrimental value of the two general rigid/ extreme attitudes and you can commit to implementing the former.

- Bring your two general flexible/non-extreme attitudes towards your performance and uncertainty related to your performance to situations where you failed to do perfectly well and consider what you did achieve as well as what you did not achieve:

  'Although I originally thought I failed, I can see that achieving 90 per cent is actually evidence that I have done very well.'

- If you did actually fail, use a specific version of your general failure-based flexible/non-extreme attitude to deal with this. For example:

  Inference: *'I actually failed the test.'*

  Specific flexible/non-extreme attitude: *'I did not want to fail this test, but that does not mean that I absolutely should not have done so. Failing the test is bad, but I am not a failure. I am a unique, unrateable, fallible human being capable of failing and succeeding.'*

How to examine the accuracy of your inference of loss, failure or undeserved plight, if necessary

If you are still unsure if you have experienced a loss, failure or undeserved plight, answer one or more of the following questions (which focus on failure to exemplify the points made):

- How valid is my conclusion that I failed (for example)?

- Would an objective jury agree that I failed? If not, what would the jury's verdict be?

- Is my conclusion that I failed realistic? If not, what is a more realistic conclusion?

- If I asked someone whom I could trust to give me an objective opinion about my conclusion that I failed, what would the person say to me and why? What conclusion would this person encourage me to make instead?

- If a friend had told me that they had made the same conclusion that they had failed, what would I say to them about the validity of their conclusion and why? What conclusion would I encourage this friend to make instead?

Assessing and dealing with emotional problems about depression

In Chapter 2, I discussed the concept of meta-disturbance (literally disturbance about disturbance). It is important to assess carefully the nature of this meta-disturbance about depression before you can best deal with it.

The best way to start dealing with the assessment of any emotional problems you might have about depression is to ask yourself the question: 'How do I feel about being depressed?' The most common emotional problems that people have about depression are as follows: anxiety, depression, guilt, unhealthy regret, shame and unhealthy self-anger. I discuss only the second of these in this chapter, i.e., depression about depression, and refer you to the respective chapters on anxiety, guilt, unhealthy regret, shame and unhealthy anger for how to deal with these emotional problems as applied to depression.

Assessing depression about depression

When you are depressed about depression, it is clear that you think of your original depression as a loss, failure or undeserved plight. The most common of these inferences are as follows:

- Depression means that I have lost connection with people (in the sociotropic realm).

- Depression means that I have to rely on others (in the autonomic realm).

- Depression is an additional undeserved burden I have to deal with (in the undeservingness realm).

Dealing with depression about depression

Unless you deal with your depression about depression (called meta-depression), you are unlikely to deal with your original depression, since your meta-depression will lead you to focus on themes about which you are likely to feel even more depressed. Thus, meta-depression (if you experience it) often has to be dealt with before you deal with your original depression.

As I have made clear in this book, it is important that you develop and apply flexible/non-extreme attitudes towards loss, failure and undeserved plight, while becoming more active and while letting be (i.e., not engaging with or distracting yourself from) any remaining post-rigid/extreme attitude negative thoughts or images you may have. With these points in mind, let me give you brief advice of how to deal with the three forms of depression about depression I have listed.

Dealing with the loss of connection with others

This is an issue that you are more likely to have if your depression is in the sociotropic realm than in the autonomous or undeservingness realms. In order to deal with this issue, you need to do the following. First, develop a set of flexible/non-extreme attitudes towards the loss of connection with others (after examining both your rigid/extreme and flexible/non-extreme attitudes as outlined in Appendices 2–5). These may be ego in nature (e.g., 'I would prefer not to lose connection with others, but that does not mean it must not happen. If it does, that is unfortunate, but it does not prove I am unlovable. I am a unique, unrateable person who is capable of being loved whether I am connected to others or not') or non-ego in nature (e.g., 'I would prefer not to lose connection with others, but that does not mean it must not happen. If it does, it is a struggle for me to put up with this uncomfortable situation, but I can tolerate it and it is worth it to me to do so'). Then, it's useful for you to develop a shorthand version of these flexible/non-extreme attitudes (e.g., 'Connection with others is good, but not necessary') and use this before seeking to reconnect with others and as you do so.

Dealing with relying on others

When you are depressed, you may lose some autonomy and be forced to rely on others. This is a particular problem for those who are rigid about having autonomy. If you are likely to make yourself depressed about having to rely on others, this is what you need to do. First, develop a set of flexible/non-extreme attitudes towards having to rely on others (after examining both your rigid/extreme and flexible/non-extreme attitudes as outlined in Appendices 2–5). Again, these may be ego in nature (e.g., 'I would prefer not to rely on others, but I do not always have my wish fulfilled on this issue. If I do have to rely on others, this does not prove I am a weak person. I am a fallible person whose worth does not change if I have to rely on others') or non-ego in nature (e.g., 'I would prefer not to rely on others, but I do not always have to have my wish fulfilled on this issue. If I do have to rely on others, that's unfortunate, but it isn't terrible'). Then, it's again useful to develop a shorthand version of these flexible/non-extreme attitudes (e.g., 'I am fallible, not weak, if I have to rely on others') and use this before seeking help from others and as you do so.

Dealing with the additional burden of depression

The first step in dealing with this depression is to assume temporarily that depression is an additional burden. Then, develop a set of flexible/non-extreme attitudes towards having such undeserved plight (after examining both your rigid/extreme and flexible/non-extreme attitudes as outlined in Appendices 2–4). These are likely to be non-ego in nature (e.g., 'I would prefer not to have this additional undeserved burden on me, but that does not mean that I must not have it. It is unfortunate that I have it, but not terrible and I am not a poor person as a result. I am a non-poor person in a poor situation'). Once again, it's useful to develop a shorthand version of this flexible/non-extreme attitude (e.g., 'Depression is poor, but I'm not') and use this before tackling your original depression.

Developing and rehearsing non-depressed, sadness-based world views

People develop views of the world as it relates to them that make it more or less likely that they will experience UNEs. The world views that render you vulnerable to depression do so in a similar way to your general rigid/extreme attitudes towards a specific loss, failure or undeserved plight theme by making you focus unduly on the presence of loss, failure or undeserved plight about which you hold depression-related rigid/extreme attitudes. However, these depression-based world views have this effect on you much more widely.

It is important that you develop realistic views of the world that will help you to deal with depression and experience healthy sadness instead. In Table 3.1, you will find an illustrative list of such world views rather than an exhaustive one, so you can get an idea of what I mean, which will enable you to develop your own. In Table 3.1, I first describe a world view

Table 3.1 World views that render you vulnerable to depression and help you to deal with depression

Views of the world that render you vulnerable to depression	Views of the world that help you deal with depression
◉ The world is a bad place	◉ The world is a place where bad, good and neutral things happen
◉ Life is ultimately meaningless	◉ Life neither has meaning nor is meaningless. I can find and actively pursue a number of meaningful projects over my life-span
◉ People will ultimately reject me, therefore it is best not be get involved with them	◉ Some people will reject me, others will not. I can actively involve myself in relationships in light of this fact
◉ People cannot be trusted	◉ People vary enormously along a continuum of trustworthiness. My best stance is to trust someone unless I have evidence to the contrary. If I am let down that is very unfortunate, but hardly terrible and won't unduly affect my stance towards the next person I meet
◉ The world is made up of strong and weak people	◉ The world is made up of people who all have their strengths and weaknesses

that renders you vulnerable to depression and then I give its healthy alternative. You will see that the latter views are characterised by complexity and being non-extreme in nature, whereas, in the former, aspects of the world that relate to loss, failure and undeserved plight are portrayed as unidimensional and extreme.

If you hold flexible/non-extreme attitudes that are consistent with the views of the world listed on the right-hand side of Table 3.1, and if you act and think in ways that are, in turn, consistent with these flexible/non-extreme attitudes, you will become less prone to depression.

In Chapter 4, I discuss guilt and how to deal with it.

NOTES

1 In this chapter, I am talking about non-clinical depression. Clinical depression is characterised by a number of biological features such as insomnia, loss of appetite, loss of libido and suicidal ideation. If you think you may be clinically depressed, consult your GP in the first instance.
2 When I discuss undeserved plight in this chapter, I am referring to such plight that can befall you and/or others. This is the major theme in pity-based depression.

Dealing with guilt

In this chapter, I begin by presenting REBT's way of understanding guilt and then address how to deal with this emotional problem.

UNDERSTANDING GUILT

In understanding guilt, we need to know what we tend to make ourselves guilty about (i.e., its major inference themes), what attitudes we hold, how we act or tend to act, and how we think when we are feeling guilty.

Major inference themes in guilt

There are three major themes in relation to your personal domain that are implicated in guilt:

⊚ You have broken your moral code (i.e., you have done the wrong thing).

⊚ You have failed to live up to your moral code (i.e., you failed to do the right thing).

⊚ You have hurt someone's feelings.

Rigid/extreme attitudes

As I explained in Chapter 1, according to REBT, inferences on their own do not account for emotional problems. It is possible, therefore, for you to make the same inferences as listed above and be remorseful, but not guilty. In order for you to feel guilty when you think that you have done the wrong thing, failed to do the right thing or hurt someone's feelings, you have to hold a rigid/extreme attitude. In guilt, this will involve you holding a rigid attitude and an extreme self-devaluation attitude.

DOI: 10.4324/9781003424307-4

Behaviour associated with guilt

When you hold a rigid/extreme attitude towards doing the wrong thing, failing to do the right thing or hurting someone's feelings, you will act or tend to act in a number of ways, the most common of which are as follows:

- You escape from the unhealthy pain of guilt in self-defeating ways.
- You beg forgiveness from the person you have wronged.
- You promise unrealistically that you will not 'sin' again.
- You punish yourself physically or by deprivation.
- You defensively disclaim responsibility for wrongdoing.
- You reject offers of forgiveness.

You will see from the above list that these behaviours get in the way of you thinking clearly about what you did or failed to do and the reasons for this so that you can understand and learn from the situation.

Thinking associated with guilt

When you hold a rigid/extreme attitude towards doing the wrong thing, failing to do the right thing or hurting someone's feelings, you will tend to think in a number of ways. Remember what I said in Chapter 1: the thinking that accompanies your guilt is the result of your inference (i.e., that you did the wrong thing, failed to do the right thing or hurt others in some way) being processed by your rigid/extreme attitude and therefore it is likely to contain a number of thinking errors that I present in Appendix 1. I list the main features of this post-rigid/extreme attitude guilty thinking below:

- You conclude that you have definitely committed the sin.
- You assume more personal responsibility than the situation warrants.
- You assign far less responsibility to others than is warranted.
- You dismiss possible mitigating factors for your behaviour.

- You see your behaviour only in a guilt-related context and fail to put it into an overall context.

- You think that you will receive retribution.

As you can see, such thinking exaggerates the degree of responsibility you have and the negative consequences of your behaviour, and also ignores the role of context. As with post-rigid/extreme attitude anxiety thinking and depressed thinking, post-rigid/extreme attitude guilty thinking may be in words or in mental images.

HOW TO DEAL WITH GUILT

If you are prone to guilt, you tend to experience this emotional problem in a variety of different settings and in response to a variety of perceived moral code violations and failures, as well as times when you inflict hurt on others. Here is how to deal with guilt so that you become less prone to it.

Step 1: Identify reasons why guilt is a problem for you and why you want to change

While guilt is generally regarded as an emotional problem, it is useful for you to spell out reasons why guilt is a problem for you and why you want to change. I suggest that you keep a written list of these reasons and refer to it as needed as a reminder of why you are engaged in a self-help pro-gramme. I discuss the healthy alternative to guilt in Step 4.

Step 2: Take responsibility for your guilt

In REBT, we argue that what you do or don't do does not make you feel guilty; rather you create these feelings by the rigid/extreme attitudes that you hold towards what you do or don't do. Unless you accept this point, you will not address your guilt productively. Rather, you will think that the only way not to feel guilty is by always acting morally and never hurting people's feelings. This will perpetuate your guilt rather than deal with it.

Step 3: Identify the themes you tend to be guilty about

The best way of identifying guilt-related inference themes to which you are particularly vulnerable is by understanding the themes associated with guilt, and seeing which are present when you feel guilty. As I outlined above, there are three such themes:

- You have broken your moral code (i.e., you have done the wrong thing).

- You have failed to live up to your moral code (i.e., you have failed to do the right thing).

- You have hurt someone's feelings.

Step 4: Identify the three components of your guilt response and set goals with respect to each component

The next step is for you to list the three elements of your guilt response in the face of each of the relevant themes listed above.

Identify the three components of your guilt response

I use the term 'guilt response' to describe the three main components that make up this response. The three components of your guilt response are the emotional, behavioural and thinking components.

Emotional component

The emotional component here is, of course, guilt.

Behavioural component

The behavioural component concerns overt behaviour or action tendencies that you engage in or 'feel like' engaging in when you feel guilty. Consult the list that I provided to help you identify your behaviour associated with each relevant theme when you are guilty (see p. 66).

Thinking component

The thinking component associated with guilt is listed on pp. 66–67. Again, these may be in words or in mental pictures. Consult the list if necessary.

Set goals with respect to each of the three components

You need to set goals so that you know what you are striving for when you deal effectively with guilt. The three goals are emotional, behavioural and thinking goals.

Emotional goal

Your emotional goal is remorse rather than guilt (or whatever synonym you prefer to the term 'remorse'). Remorse is an HNE, which is an appropriate response to doing the wrong thing, not doing the right thing or hurting someone's feelings. It helps you to think objectively about the situation and your response to it, and helps you to move on with your life rather than get stuck or bogged down.

Behavioural goal

Your behavioural goal should reflect actions that are based on remorse about doing the wrong thing, not doing the right thing or hurting someone's feelings, rather than guilt. The following are the most common behaviours associated with remorse. You may wish to compare these behaviours with those associated with guilt that I presented on p. 66.

- You face up to the healthy pain that accompanies the realisation that you have sinned.
- You ask, but do not beg, for forgiveness.
- You understand the reasons for your wrongdoing and act on your understanding.
- You atone for the sin by taking a penalty.
- You make appropriate amends.
- You do not make excuses for your behaviour or enact other defensive behaviour.
- You accept offers of forgiveness.

Thinking goal

As well as setting behavioural goals related to the feeling of remorse about doing the wrong thing, not doing the right thing or hurting someone's feelings, it is important that you set thinking goals associated with this emotion. The following are the most common forms of thinking associated with remorse rather than guilt. Again, you may wish to compare these forms of thinking with those associated with guilt that I presented on pp. 66–67.

- You take into account all relevant data when judging whether or not you have 'sinned'.

- You assume an appropriate level of personal responsibility.

- You assign an appropriate level of responsibility to others.

- You take into account mitigating factors.

- You put your behaviour into overall context.

- You think you may be penalised rather than receive retribution.

As the above list shows, the dominant feature of thinking associated with remorse is that it is realistic and balanced. Please remember that such thinking may be in words or in mental pictures.

Step 5: Identify your general rigid/extreme attitudes and alternative general flexible/ non-extreme attitudes

A general rigid/extreme attitude leading to your guilt response is a rigid/ extreme attitude that you hold across situations defined by one of the following themes: breaking your moral code, failing to live up to your moral code or hurting someone's feelings. Its flexible/non-extreme alternative, which will also be general in nature, will account for your remorse response.

Identify your general rigid/extreme attitudes

When you identify a general rigid/extreme attitude, you take a common guilt-related theme (i.e., doing the wrong thing, failing to do the right thing or hurting someone's feelings) and add to this a general rigid attitude and the main extreme attitude that is derived from the rigid attitude. In guilt, your main extreme attitude will be a self-devaluation attitude. For example:

⦿ 'I must not hurt my family's feelings and, if I do, I am bad.'

Identify your alternative general flexible/non-extreme attitudes

When you identify your alternative general flexible/non-extreme attitude, you take the same common theme (i.e., doing the wrong thing, failing to do the right thing or hurting someone's feelings) and add to this a general flexible attitude and the main non-extreme attitude that is derived from the flexible attitude. In remorse, your main non-extreme attitude will be an unconditional self-acceptance attitude. For example:

⦿ 'I really don't want to hurt my family's feelings, but that does not mean that I must never do so. If I do, that would be bad, but it would not prove that I am bad. I am fallible and capable of doing good and bad things.'

Step 6: Examine your general attitudes

I recommended in Chapters 2 and 3 that you first examine together your general rigid attitude and its general flexible attitude alternative and then examine together your general extreme attitude and your general non-extreme attitude.

Examine your general rigid attitude and its general flexible attitude alternative

First, take your general rigid attitude and its general flexible attitude alternative and write them down next to one another on a sheet of paper. Then ask yourself:

⦿ Which is true and which is false?

⦿ Which is sensible logically and which does not make sense?

⦿ Which has largely constructive results and which has largely unconstructive results?

Write down your answer to each of these questions on your piece of paper, giving reasons for each answer. Consult Appendix 2 for help with the answers to these questions, which you need to adapt and apply to the attitudes you are examining.

Examine your general self-devaluation attitude and its general unconditional self-acceptance attitude alternative

Next, take your general self-devaluation attitude and its general unconditional self-acceptance attitude alternative and again write them down next to one another on a sheet of paper. Then, ask yourself the same three questions that you used with your general rigid attitude and its general flexible attitude alternative. Again, write down your answer to each of these questions on your piece of paper, giving your reasons for each answer. I suggest that you consult Appendix 5 (for help with examining self-devaluation attitudes and unconditional self-acceptance attitudes). Again, you need to adapt and apply these arguments to the attitudes you are examining.

You should now be ready to commit to acting and thinking in ways consistent with your general flexible/non-extreme attitude.

Step 7: Take an appropriate amount of responsibility and understand your behaviour in context

Once you have committed yourself to your general flexible/non-extreme attitude, it is important that you look again at events about which you have made yourself guilty, but this time you need to view them through the eyes of your general flexible/non-extreme attitudes (i.e., flexible and unconditional self-acceptance attitudes). This basically involves you taking responsibility for your behaviour, but recognising that others have responsibility too. It also involves you understanding your behaviour in context. This means that you need to consider the factors involved in the situation. When you feel guilt, you see things in black and white, and tend to take far too much responsibility and edit out the impact of other factors external to you. In remorse, you recognise the complexity of the situation and the fact that there are many influences on your behaviour.

As such, remorse helps you to learn from situations in which you think you have broken or failed to live up to your moral code or you have hurt someone's feelings and to use this learning in future situations.

Step 8: Face your guilt-related theme in imagery

I hope that you have made a commitment to act on your general flexible/non-extreme attitudes (i.e., flexible attitude and unconditional self-acceptance attitude). Assuming that you have, your basic task is to face up to doing the wrong thing, failing to do the right thing or hurting someone's feelings, and to learn to think flexibly and in a non-extreme way about it.

Up to this point, you have worked at a general level with respect to your guilt-related theme, dealing with the general rigid/extreme attitudes that account for your guilt and developing your alternative general flexible/non-extreme attitudes. However, when you come to apply your general flexible/non-extreme attitudes in dealing with breaking or failing to live up to your moral code or hurting someone, you need to remember one important point. Since you make yourself guilty about specific events (actual or imagined), you need to deal with these by rehearsing specific variants of your general flexible/non-extreme attitudes.

While the best way to do this is in specific situations with people who were involved when you broke your moral code, failed to live up to your moral code or whose feelings you hurt, you may derive benefit by using imagery first If this is the case, you need to do the following:

⦿ Imagine a specific situation in which you felt guilty or may feel guilty about breaking or failing to live up to your moral code or hurting someone's feelings and focus, in your mind's eye, on what you felt most guilty about (i.e., your 'A').

⦿ Focus on this 'A' while rehearsing a specific flexible/non-extreme attitude relevant to the situation. As you do this, try to make yourself feel remorseful, rather than guilty.

⦿ Then, see yourself acting in ways consistent with your flexible/non-extreme attitude, e.g., apologising, making amends and engaging the other in a productive dialogue.

⦿ Recognise that some of your post-rigid/extreme-attitude thinking may be distorted. Respond to it without getting bogged down doing so. Accept the presence of any remaining distorted thoughts without engaging with them.

⦿ Repeat the above steps until you feel sufficiently ready to put this sequence into practice in your life.

If you find that facing your guilt-related 'A', in your mind's eye, is too much for you, use the 'challenging, but not overwhelming' principle that I introduced in Chapter 2 (see p. 33). This means that, instead of imagining yourself facing a moral code violation (commission or omission) or hurting someone's feelings that you find 'overwhelming' at the present time, choose a similar guilt-related 'A' that you would find 'challenging, but not overwhelming'. Then employ the same steps that I have outlined above. Work in this way with modified guilt-related 'A's' until you find your original one 'challenging, but not overwhelming' and then use the steps again.

Step 9: Apologise, make amends and talk things through

Once you have understood your behaviour in context and taken responsibility for what you are in fact responsible for, you are in a position to act on this. This may mean apologising to relevant others for your behaviour and/or making amends to them in some way. Whatever action you need to take, you first need to get into a flexible/non-extreme frame of mind. When you feel remorseful, but not guilty, you are encouraged to engage others in a productive dialogue about the situation in question, if they are amenable to doing so. The purpose of this dialogue is mutual understanding and reconciliation.

Step 10: Capitalise on what you have learned

When you have faced a situation in which you experienced guilt and dealt with it as best you could, it is important that you reflect on what you did and what you learned. In particular, if you were able to face the situation, and rehearse your specific flexible/non-extreme attitudes until you felt remorse, then ask yourself how you can capitalise on what you achieved. If you experienced any problems, respond to the following questions:

⊙ Did I face the situation and, if not, why not?

⊙ Did I rehearse my flexible/non-extreme attitudes before, during or after facing the situation and, if not, why not?

⊙ Did I execute my plan to face the situation and, if not, why not?

◉ Did I engage with post-rigid/extreme attitude distorted thinking and, if so, why?

Reflect on your experience and put into practice what you have learned the next time you face a situation in which you consider that you acted in a way you wished you had not acted or failed to act in a way you wished you had acted.

Step 11: Generalise your learning

Once you have dealt with your guilt in a specific situation by holding the relevant specific version of your general flexible/non-extreme attitude, and by acting and thinking in ways that are consistent with it, you can generalise this learning to situations defined by you breaking or failing to live up to your moral code or hurting others' feelings.

Billy was particularly prone to guilt about hurting others' feelings, so he followed the steps outlined in this chapter. Thus:

◉ Billy assessed the three components of his guilt response and set goals with respect to all three components.

◉ He identified his relevant general rigid/extreme attitude regarding hurting others' feelings (i.e., 'I must not hurt people's feelings and, if I do, I'm a bad person') that underpinned his guilt response and his alternative general flexible/non-extreme attitude (i.e., 'I don't want to hurt people's feelings, but I am not immune to doing so and nor do I have to be so immune. If I do hurt others' feelings it is bad, but I am not a bad person. I am an ordinary fallible person who has done something bad') that underpinned his remorse response.

◉ He examined both elements of his general rigid/extreme attitude and his general flexible/non-extreme attitude until he clearly saw that the former were false, made no sense and were detrimental to him, and that the latter were true, sensible and healthy.

◉ He thought about what he was actually responsible for and what others were responsible for and saw that there were other factors involved that he did not take into account when he felt guilty, which need to be factored in and understood. Then he met with these others, apologised and made amends when he needed to, and talked things through with them.

⊙ As he did so, he tolerated the discomfort that he felt and accepted that some of his distorted and skewed negative thinking would still be in his mind. He let such thinking be without engaging with it, suppressing it or distracting himself from it.

As this section shows, you can generalise what you learn about dealing with guilt from situation to situation as defined by your moral code violation, failure to live up to that code or by hurting others' feelings. If you do this, you will take the toxicity out of the emotional problem of guilt!

USING REBT'S ABCD FORM TO DEAL WITH SPECIFIC EXAMPLES OF YOUR GUILT

This chapter is mainly geared to help you deal with your guilt in general terms. However, you can also use this material to address specific examples of your guilt. I have developed a self-help form to provide the structure to assist you in this regard. It is called the ABCD form and it appears with instructions in Appendix 6.

OTHER IMPORTANT ISSUES IN DEALING WITH GUILT

In the above section, I outlined an 11-step programme to deal with guilt. In this section, I discuss some other important issues that may be relevant to you in your work to become less prone to this emotional problem. If you want to, you can incorporate them as additional steps in the above step-by-step guide at points relevant to you.

Dealing with your safety-seeking measures to avoid guilt

I mentioned in Chapter 2 that people use safety-seeking measures to protect themselves from threat. You may use similar measures to protect yourself from feeling guilty. Here is how this works from your perspective. You reason that, since you feel guilty about (a) doing the wrong thing, (b) failing to do the right thing and (c) hurting people's feelings, you will take steps to avoid guilt by always doing the right thing and never hurting people's feelings. Taking this decision means that you will not take risks in life (in case you do the wrong thing or upset others, for example), always put others first (so that others are not upset) and go out of your way to get people to like you (again, to ensure that you do not upset them).

However, this behaviour and the reasoning that leads you to take it are flawed and will serve only to perpetuate your chronic guilt. This is due to the fact that your guilt is based not on you (a) doing the wrong thing, (b) failing to do the right thing and (c) hurting people's feelings, but on your rigid/extreme attitudes towards these three inferences. So, if you want to deal effectively with guilt, you need to do the following:

- Take healthy risks, put yourself first again in a healthy way and stop going out of your way to get people to like you, and see what happens. You will probably find that people are not upset as much as you think and that you have not broken any of your moral codes.

- However, if, as a result of your behaviour, you do break one of your moral codes, fail to live up to them or upset others, then you can deal with such situations by holding a set of flexible/non-extreme attitudes towards them so that you feel healthy remorse and not unhealthy guilt about these consequences.

Why you feel guilty much of the time and how to deal with this

If you are particularly prone to guilt, you will think that you often do the wrong thing, fail to do the right thing or hurt the feelings of others. You do this because you hold the following attitude, which I call a 'chronic guilt-based general rigid/extreme attitude':

- 'Whenever I am involved, I must make sure that nothing bad happens or others' feelings are not hurt. If I don't and bad things happen and others are upset, then it is all my fault and I am a bad person.'

You then take this attitude to relevant situations and, even where your involvement is minimal, you think that you are at fault if there is a bad outcome. As a result, you constantly think that you are responsible for any negative outcomes that happen or might happen and end up by blaming yourself.

How to deal with chronic guilt

In order to deal with this chronic sense of guilt, you need to develop and apply an alternative general flexible/non-extreme attitude that protects you from such guilt:

- 'Whenever I am involved, I want to make sure that nothing bad happens or that others' feelings are not hurt, but I don't have to succeed in doing so. If I don't and bad things happen and others are upset, then I will take the appropriate level of responsibility, assign appropriate responsibility to others and consider the impact of situational factors. I will accept myself for failing to adhere to my code and for any hurt that I inadvertently cause.'

Such an attitude will lead you to think that you have broken your moral code, failed to adhere to the code or hurt someone's feelings only when there is clear evidence for making such an inference. When there is, you will feel remorse rather than guilt because you will be processing this with a specific flexible/non-extreme attitude.

How to examine the accuracy of your guilt-related inference, if necessary

If you are still unsure if you have broken your moral code, failed to live up to it or hurt someone's feelings, answer one or more of the following questions:

- How valid is my inference that I broke my moral code (for example)?

- Would an objective jury agree that I broke my moral code? If not, what would the jury's verdict be?

- Is my inference that I broke my moral code realistic? If not, what is a more realistic inference?

- If I asked someone whom I could trust to give me an objective opinion about my inference that I broke my moral code, what would the person say to me and why? What inference would this person encourage me to make instead?

- If a friend had told me that they had made the same inference about breaking their moral code in the same situation, what would I say to them about the validity of their inference and why? What inference would I encourage this friend to make instead?

Dealing with failure to practise healthy self-care

People who have a chronic problem with guilt find it very hard to practise healthy self-care. The reason for this is as follows. Healthy self-care involves you putting yourself first unless others' needs are truly more important than your own. People with a chronic guilt problem generally think that others' needs are more important than their own and that to put oneself first is being selfish, which, if you have a chronic problem, you will seek to avoid. Putting others first helps you both to avoid considering yourself a bad person if you do put yourself first and to feel virtuous.

How to practise healthy self-care

In order to practise healthy self-care, you need to do the following:

- Develop a healthy general flexible/non-extreme attitude that underpins the practice of healthy self-care (e.g., 'I am a fallible human being and if I don't look after myself, nobody will. I am not a bad person if I put myself first even though doing this is uncomfortable').

- Put this into practice and rehearse shortened specific versions of this general flexible/non-extreme attitude before you take self-caring action, while you do so and after you have done so.

- Recognise that this will feel very uncomfortable because it will be unfamiliar. However, if you bear this discomfort and keep acting in ways that are consistent with your healthy general flexible/non-extreme attitude, then this discomfort will subside and eventually practising healthy self-care will become the familiar position for you.

Identifying and dealing with the hidden conceit in guilt

It may sound strange, but, when you think about guilt from a particular perspective, an attitude of hidden conceit is revealed. Such conceit is revealed when you are asked to judge someone who has acted in a situation in the same way as you. Let me give an example to make this clear.

June felt guilty whenever she said 'No' to her mother, even when the latter made unreasonable requests on June, as she increasingly did. June's general rigid/extreme attitude with respect to her mother was: 'I must make my mother happy and I am bad if I don't.' June's friend Harriet also had a problem saying 'No' to her own mother and whenever she discussed her guilt and helplessness with June, June advised Harriet to think more of herself and lay down boundaries with her mother. This was precisely what June did not do for herself. June's view of Harriet was that she was a fallible human being with limitations who had to lay down healthy boundaries to deal with this complex situation. June's view of herself was that she should be a good daughter, strong enough to cope with the demands of her mother, and that she was bad if she did not. June's hidden conceit is thus revealed in her differential expectations of herself and Harriet. She sees Harriet as fallible with limitations. She sees herself as someone who should be able to cope with a situation that she does not expect Harriet to be able to cope with. This 'holier than thou' attitude is common in guilt: 'I must be thoroughly good and, if I'm not, I'm bad.'

It is very important that you deal with this hidden conceit if you want to become less prone to guilt. You do this in ways that should now be familiar to you:

⊙ By all means have high standards for yourself in the moral realm of the personal domain, but remind yourself that you don't always have to achieve these standards.

⊙ Accept yourself as a fallible human being with limitations in the same way as you would others. Self-compassion is crucial here and I recommend the writings of Paul Gilbert on this subject (e.g., *The Compassionate Mind*, 2009).

Can you hurt the feelings of others?

Throughout this chapter, I have used terms such as 'hurting people's feelings'. I have done so because this is how people prone to guilt tend to think. When you think that you have hurt someone's feelings, this is an inference and, as we have seen in this book, people's emotional problems are not determined by inferences alone, they are largely determined by the rigid/extreme attitudes that they hold towards these inferences. Thus, you don't feel guilty because you think you have hurt someone's feelings, you feel guilty because you hold a rigid/extreme attitude towards this inference. So, to deal with guilt, you need to assume temporarily that you did, in fact, hurt someone's feelings so that you can identify and deal effectively with your guilt-inducing rigid/extreme attitudes.

When you have done this and are looking back at the event with your flexible/non-extreme mind, it is useful to consider the question: 'Can I, in reality, hurt the feelings of others?' From the perspective of REBT, the answer is 'No'. As I will explain in Chapter 6, when a person feels hurt about someone's behaviour, they do so because they hold a rigid/extreme attitude towards that person's behaviour. So, when you say that you have hurt someone's feelings, you are working on the assumption that your behaviour directly makes the other person feel hurt. You are implying that the person's attitudes play no part in this, which is patently false. So, it is important that you don't take responsibility for the other person's feelings. That does not mean that you can treat another person badly, safe in the knowledge that you aren't responsible for that person's feelings. Far from it!

What I am suggesting is that, while you should not take responsibility for the feelings of others, you should take full responsibility for the way you treat others. However, taking full responsibility for your behaviour does not mean that you have to blame yourself if you do treat someone badly, for responsibility is not synonymous with blame. If you do treat someone badly, it is healthy for you to feel remorse about that, an emotion based on a flexible/non-extreme attitude that will help you to stand back and learn from the experience so you are less likely to act that way in future.

Assessing and dealing with emotional problems about guilt

In previous chapters, I discussed the concept of meta-disturbance (literally disturbance about disturbance). It is important to assess carefully the nature of this meta-disturbance about guilt before you can best deal with it.

The best way to start dealing with the assessment of any emotional problems you might have about guilt is to ask yourself the question: 'How do I feel about my feeling of guilt?' The most common emotional problems that people have about guilt are as follows: anxiety, depression, unhealthy regret, shame and unhealthy self-anger. As it is unlikely that you will feel guilty about feeling guilty, I refer you to the chapters on anxiety, depression, unhealthy regret, shame and unhealthy anger for help on how to deal with these meta-emotional problems about guilt.

Developing and rehearsing non-guilt, remorse-based world views

People develop views of the world as it relates to them that make it more or less likely that they will experience UNEs. The world views that render you vulnerable to guilt do so in a similar way to the chronic guilt-based general rigid/extreme attitude discussed above (i.e., 'Whenever I am involved, I must make sure that nothing bad happens or others' feelings are not hurt. If I don't, it is all my fault and I am a bad person') by making you focus unduly on things you have done that you think are wrong, your failures to do the right thing and the hurt you think you have caused others. However, these guilt-based world views have this effect on you much more widely.

It is important that you develop realistic views of the world that will help you to deal with guilt and experience remorse instead. In Table 4.1, you will find an illustrative list of such world views rather than an exhaustive one, so you can get an idea of what I mean, which will enable you to develop your own. In Table 4.1, I first describe a world view that renders you vulnerable to guilt and then I give its healthy alternatives You will see that the latter views are characterised by the idea that you are as important and as fallible as others, whereas, in the former, you are less important and more responsible than others.

If you hold flexible/non-extreme attitudes that are consistent with the views of the world listed on the right-hand side of Table 4.1, and if you act and think in ways that are, in turn, consistent with these flexible/non-extreme attitudes, you will become less prone to guilt.

In Chapter 5, I discuss unhealthy regret and how to deal with it.

Table 4.1 World views that render you vulnerable to guilt and help you to deal with guilt

Views of the world that render you vulnerable to guilt	Views of the world that help you deal with guilt
⊚ Other people's desires are more important than my own	⊚ My desires are no less important to me than others' desires are to them. I can flexibly and healthily prioritise my desires in the same way as others can flexibly and healthily prioritise theirs
⊚ When I am involved I have responsibility for the hurt feelings of others.	⊚ When I am involved, I have responsibility for my actions, but ultimately I am not responsible for the feelings of others. They are responsible
⊚ In the moral domain, I expect more of myself than I do of others	⊚ In the moral domain, I can expect the same of myself as I can expect of others
⊚ It is possible to always act morally	⊚ It is rarely possible to always act morally since, if you do the right thing from one perspective, you may be doing the wrong thing from another perspective
⊚ Saying 'No' to others is a sign of selfishness	⊚ Saying 'No' to others may be selfish, but is more likely to be a sign of healthy self-care

Dealing with unhealthy regret

In this chapter, I begin by presenting REBT's way of understanding unhealthy regret and then address how to deal with this emotional problem.

UNDERSTANDING UNHEALTHY REGRET

In understanding unhealthy regret, we need to know what we tend to make ourselves unhealthily regretful about (i.e., its major inference themes), what attitudes we hold, how we act or tend to act, and how we think when we are feeling unhealthy regret.

   There are, in my view, two forms of regret: retrospective regret where you are regretful about matters in the past and prospective regret where you are mindful of what you may regret in the future, which impacts on your present behaviour and future.

Major inference themes in unhealthy regret

There are two major themes in relation to your personal domain that are implicated in unhealthy retrospective regret:

⦿ You took action in the past and wished you had not done so.

⦿ You failed to take action in the past and wished you had done so.

There is one major theme in relation to your personal domain that is implicated in unhealthy prospective regret:

⦿ You face uncertainty about the consequences of taking action now or in the future.

DOI: 10.4324/9781003424307-5

Rigid/extreme attitudes

As I explained in Chapter 1, according to REBT, inferences on their own do not account for emotional problems. It is possible, therefore, for you to make the same inferences as listed above and be healthily regretful, but not unhealthily regretful. In order for you to feel unhealthy regret about taking action in the past and wishing you had not done so, failing to take action in the past and wishing you had done so and about the uncertainty you face about making a decision[1] now or in the future, you have to hold a rigid/extreme attitude.

Behaviour associated with unhealthy regret

When you hold a rigid/extreme attitude towards taking action in the past and wishing you had not done so, failing to take action in the past and wishing you had done so and towards the uncertainty you face about making a decision now or in the future, you will act or tend to act in a number of ways.

When you are focused on the past in unhealthy retrospective regret:

- You review physical evidence in the hope of finding something that you missed at the time that would have led you to have made the best decision[2] and not stopping until you feel at ease.

- You seek reassurance from others that the best decision was made, but do not feel reassured.

When you are focused on the present/future in unhealthy prospective regret:

- You review physical evidence in order to find the best decision possible and feel certain that you have done so, and you don't stop until you have done so to your satisfaction.

- You do more research until you have gotten all possible information so that you can be certain that you can make the best decision.

- You seek guidance from others about what is the best decision you can make until you feel certain that have found it.

- You are indecisive.

You will see from the above list that these behaviours get in the way of you thinking clearly about what you did or what you failed to do and the reasons for this so that you can understand and learn from the situation.

Thinking associated with unhealthy regret

When you hold a rigid/extreme attitude towards taking action in the past and wishing you had not done so, failing to take action in the past and wishing you had done so and towards the uncertainty you face about making a decision now or in the future, you will tend to think in a number of ways. Remember what I said in Chapter 1: the thinking that accompanies your unhealthy regret is the result of your inference (i.e., that you took action in the past and wished you had not done so, failed to take action in the past and wished you had done so and face uncertainty about making a decision now or in the future), is being processed by your rigid/extreme attitude and therefore it is likely to contain a number of thinking errors that I present in Appendix 1. I list the main features of this post-rigid/extreme attitude unhealthy regret thinking below. Please note that all these thinking consequences are ruminative in nature.

When you are focused on the past in unhealthy retrospective regret:

⊚ You revisit the decision in your mind with the purpose of discovering what would have led you to have made the best decision possible and you criticise yourself for not knowing what it was and for thereby making the wrong decision.[3]

⊚ You are sure that you made the wrong decision.

⊚ You engage in if-only thinking. You are sure that, if you had taken a different course of action, your life would have taken a much better course.

When you are focused on the present/future in unhealthy prospective regret:

⊚ You review all the evidence in your mind until you are sure that you have made the best decision, but without ever achieving such certainty.

⊚ You think that you have missed something crucial, but do not know what it is and you search for the missing ingredient in your mind until you have found it.

As you can see, such thinking exaggerates the negative consequences of your behaviour and also ignores the role of context. Post-rigid/extreme attitude unhealthy regret thinking may be in words or in mental images.

HOW TO DEAL WITH UNHEALTHY REGRET

If you are prone to unhealthy regret, you tend to experience this emotional problem in a variety of different settings and in response to a variety of instances where you took action in the past and wished you had not done so, failed to take action in the past and wished you had done so and when you are uncertain about making a decision now or in the future. Here is how to deal with unhealthy regret so that you become less prone to it.

Step 1: Identify which type of unhealthy regret you experience and the reasons why unhealthy regret is a problem for you and why you want to change

While unhealthy regret is generally regarded as an emotional problem, it is useful for you first to be clear with yourself whether you are experiencing unhealthy retrospective regret or unhealthy prospective regret. If you experience both, you need to deal with them one at a time. Then, you need to spell out reasons why unhealthy regret is a problem for you and why you want to change. I suggest that you keep a written list of these reasons and refer to it as needed as a reminder of why you are engaged in a self-help programme. I discuss the healthy alternative to unhealthy regret in Step 4.

Step 2: Take responsibility for your unhealthy regret

In REBT, we argue that what you do or don't do does not make you feel unhealthy regret; rather, you create these feelings through the rigid/ extreme attitudes that you hold towards what you do or don't do. Unless you accept this point, you will not address your unhealthy regret productively. Rather, you will think that the only way not to feel unhealthy regret is by always ensuring that you made the right decision in the past and that you will do so now and in the future.

Step 3: Identify the themes you tend to be unhealthily regretful about

The best way of identifying unhealthy regret-related inference themes to which you are particularly vulnerable is by understanding the themes associated with unhealthy regret, and seeing which are present when you feel unhealthy regret. As I outlined above, there are three such themes: Themes in unhealthy retrospective regret:

⊙ You took action in the past and wished you had not done so.

⊙ You failed to take action in the past and wished you had done so.

Theme in unhealthy prospective regret:

⊙ You face uncertainty about the consequences of taking action now or in the future.

Step 4: Identify the three components of your unhealthy regret response and set goals with respect to each component

The next step is for you to list the three elements of your unhealthy regret response in the face of each of the relevant themes listed above.

Identify the three components of your unhealthy regret response

I use the term 'unhealthy regret response' to describe the three main components that make up this response. The three components of your unhealthy regret response are the emotional, behavioural and thinking components.

Emotional component

The emotional component here is, of course, unhealthy regret.

Behavioural component

The behavioural component concerns overt behaviour or action tendencies that you engage in or 'feel like' engaging in when you feel unhealthy regret. Consult the list that I provided to help you identify your behaviour associated with each relevant theme when you feel unhealthy regret (see p. 85).

Thinking component

The thinking component associated with unhealthy regret is listed on p. 86. Again, these may be in words or in mental pictures. Consult the list if necessary.

Set goals with respect to each of the three components

You need to set goals so that you know what you are striving for when you deal effectively with unhealthy regret. The three goals are emotional, behavioural and thinking goals.

Emotional goal

Your emotional goal is healthy regret rather than unhealthy regret (or whatever synonym you prefer for the term 'healthy regret'). Healthy regret is an HNE, which is an appropriate response to taking action in the past and wishing you had not done so, failing to take action in the past and wishing you had done so or to the uncertainty you face about making a decision now or in the future. It helps you to think objectively about the situation and your response to it and helps you to move on with your life rather than get stuck or bogged down.

Behavioural goal

Your behavioural goal should reflect actions that are based on healthy regret about taking action in the past and wishing you had not done so, failing to take action in the past and wishing you had done so or being uncertain about making a decision now or in the future, rather than unhealthy regret. The following are the most common behaviours associated with healthy regret. You may wish to compare these behaviours with those associated with unhealthy regret that I presented on p. 85.

In healthy retrospective regret:

- If you come across physical evidence pertaining to the past decision, you do not review this as it will not change the past.
- You tell others, if relevant, what you did or did not do and why you acted or failed to act in the way that you did.

In healthy prospective regret:

- You review physical evidence in order to find the option that will yield the best outcome, but without needing to feel certain about this.
- You realise that more research is always possible, but decide not to do that research and to make a choice of action based on the available evidence.
- You share your thinking with others for their feedback and to make any changes based on that feedback, but you do not need to feel certain about the outcome of your decision.
- You make a decision when it is right for you to do so.

Thinking goal

As well as setting behavioural goals related to the feeling of healthy regret about taking action in the past and wishing you had not done so, failing to take action in the past and wishing you had done so or being uncertain about making a decision now or in the future, it is important that you set thinking goals associated with this emotion. The following are the most common forms of thinking associated with healthy regret rather than unhealthy regret. Again, you may wish to compare these forms of thinking with those associated with unhealthy regret that I presented on p. 86.

In healthy retrospective regret:

- If you revisit the decision in your mind, you remind yourself that you acted according to the information that was available at the time and that was the best you could have done.
- You recognise that there is no way of knowing if you made the right or wrong decision. You made a decision that you thought was right at the time.

⊚ You recognise that, if you had acted differently, your life may have been better, it may have been worse or it may have made no difference.

In healthy prospective regret:

⊚ You review all the evidence and then make a decision based on the probability, not certainty, that you have chosen wisely.

⊚ You recognise that you may have missed something crucial, but accept that possibility and do not delay making a decision.

As the above list shows, the dominant feature of thinking associated with healthy regret is that it is non-ruminative, realistic and balanced. Please remember that such thinking may be in words or in mental pictures.

Step 5: Identify your general rigid/extreme attitudes and alternative general flexible/ non-extreme attitudes

A general rigid/extreme attitude leading to your unhealthy regret response is a rigid/extreme attitude that you hold across situations defined by one of the following themes: taking action in the past and wishing you had not done so, failing to take action in the past and wishing you had done so or being uncertain about making a decision now or in the future. Its flexible/ non-extreme alternative, which will also be general in nature, will account for your healthy regret response.

Identify your general rigid/extreme attitudes

When you identify a general rigid/extreme attitude, you take a common unhealthy regret-related theme (i.e., taking action in the past and wishing you had not done so, failing to take action in the past and wishing you had done so or being uncertain about making a decision now or in the future) and add to this a general rigid attitude and the main extreme attitude that is derived from the rigid attitude. In unhealthy regret, your main extreme attitude may be an awfulising attitude, an unbearability attitude and/or a self-devaluation attitude. For example, in unhealthy retrospective regret this might be:

⊚ 'I absolutely should not have taken the course of action that I did back then and it is terrible that I did.'

Identify your alternative general flexible/non-extreme attitudes

When you identify your alternative general flexible/non-extreme attitude, you take the same common theme (i.e., taking action in the past and wishing you had not done so, failing to take action in the past and wishing you had done so or being uncertain about making a decision now or in the future) and add to this a general flexible attitude and the main non-extreme attitude that is derived from the flexible attitude. In healthy regret, your main non-extreme attitude will be a non-awfulising attitude, a bearability attitude and/or an unconditional self-acceptance attitude. For example, in healthy retrospective regret this might be:

⊚ I wish I had not taken the course of action that I did back then, but that does not mean that I absolutely should not have done so. It is unfortunate that I did so, but it is not terrible.'

Step 6: Examine your general attitudes

I recommended in previous chapters that you first examine together your general rigid attitude and its general flexible attitude alternative and then examine together your general extreme attitude and your general non-extreme attitude.

Examine your general rigid attitude and its general flexible attitude alternative

First, take your general rigid attitude and its general flexible attitude alternative and write them down next to one another on a sheet of paper. Then ask yourself:

⊚ Which is true and which is false?

⊚ Which is sensible logically and which does not make sense?

⊚ Which has largely constructive results and which has largely unconstructive results?

Write down your answer to each of these questions on your piece of paper,
giving reasons for each answer. Consult Appendix 2 for help with the
answers to these questions, which you need to adapt and apply to the
attitudes you are examining.

Examine your relevant general extreme attitude and its general non-extreme attitude alternative

Next, take your general extreme attitude (e.g., awfulising attitude,
unbearability attitude or self-devaluation attitude) and its general non-
extreme attitude alternative (e.g., non-awfulising attitude, bearability
attitude or unconditional self-acceptance attitude) and again write them
down next to one another on a sheet of paper. Then, ask yourself the
same three questions that you used with your general rigid attitude and
its general flexible attitude alternative. Again, write down your answer to
each of these questions on your piece of paper, giving your reasons for
each answer. I suggest that you consult Appendix 3 (for help with examining awfulising attitudes and non-awfulising attitudes), Appendix 4 (for
help with examining unbearability attitudes and bearability attitudes) and
Appendix 5 (for help with examining devaluation attitudes and unconditional acceptance attitudes). Again, you need to adapt and apply these
arguments to the attitudes you are examining.

You should now be ready to commit to acting and thinking in ways consistent with your general flexible/non-extreme attitude.

Step 7: Dispel the myth of the perfect decision solution and understand your behaviour in context

Once you have committed yourself to your general flexible/non-extreme
attitude, it is important that you do the following.

In retrospective regret

Look back at events about which you have made yourself unhealthily
regretful, but this time view them through the eyes of your general flex-
ible/non-extreme attitudes. Recognise that your decision was based on

the information that was available to you at the time and, even if you failed to use some of that information, that was the reality. When you feel unhealthy retrospective regret, you are demanding that you absolutely should have known what you did not know and made a decision that would have turned out well for you. This implies that you could see into the future and gauge with accuracy the outcome of all the different courses of action open to you and select the right one. In other words, you are demanding perfect conditions, which would have enabled you to make a perfect decision that, in turn, would have yielded a perfect outcome.

In healthy retrospective regret, you recognise the complexity of the situation and the fact that there are many influences on your behaviour. Thus, back then, you were in the position of choosing a course of action in the face of many complex variables. If you can stand back and be humble, you will see that making perfect decisions is usually not possible. As such, healthy retrospective regret helps you to learn from situations in which you think you may have made a mistake in deciding to take a course or not to take a course of action and to use this learning in future situations.

In prospective regret

Here, recognise that your job is to consider the information at your disposal before making a decision and that, if you wait for certainty or postpone making your decision by getting even more information, then you are choosing to delay, which is also an option and one that will probably yield the worst outcome for you.

Step 8: Face your unhealthy regret-related theme in imagery

I hope that you have made a commitment to act on your general flexible/non-extreme attitudes. Assuming that you have, your basic task is to face up to taking action in the past and wishing you had not done so, failing to take action in the past and wishing you had done so or being uncertain about making a decision now or in the future and to learn to think flexibly and in a non-extreme way about your particular theme.

Up to this point, you have worked at a general level with respect to your unhealthy regret-related theme, dealing with the general rigid/extreme attitudes that account for your unhealthy regret and developing your alternative general flexible/non-extreme attitudes. However, when you come to apply your general flexible/non-extreme attitudes in dealing with taking action in the past and wishing you had not done so, failing to take action in the past and wishing you had done so or being uncertain about making a decision now or in the future, you need to remember one important point. Since you make yourself unhealthily regretful about specific events (actual or imagined), you need to deal with these by rehearsing specific variants of your general flexible/non-extreme attitudes.

Since unhealthy regret largely involves your relationship with that part of you that made or may make the wrong decision, you will derive benefit from using imagery while you face these specific situations. In doing so:

◉ Imagine a specific situation in which you felt unhealthy regret or may feel unhealthy regret about taking action in the past and wishing you had not done so, failing to take action in the past and wishing you had done so or being uncertain about making a decision now or in the future and focus, in your mind's eye, on what you felt most unhealthy regret about (i.e., your 'A').

◉ Focus on this 'A' while rehearsing a specific flexible/non-extreme attitude relevant to the situation. As you do this, try to make yourself feel healthily regretful, rather than unhealthily regretful.

◉ Then, see yourself acting in ways consistent with your flexible/non-extreme attitude, e.g., telling people that while you may have made the wrong decision in the past you have decided to let that go and will go forward with a new flexible approach to making important decisions or making a decision in the present and telling people what you have done.

◉ Recognise that some of your post-rigid/extreme-attitude thinking may be distorted. Respond to it without getting bogged down doing so. Accept the presence of any remaining distorted thoughts without engaging with them.

◉ Repeat the above steps until you feel sufficiently ready to put this sequence into practice in your life.

If you find that facing your unhealthy regret-related 'A', in your mind's eye, is too much for you, use the 'challenging, but not overwhelming' principle that I introduced in Chapter 2 (see p. 33). This means that, instead of imagining yourself facing a situation where you, for example, made a decision that you think turned out very badly, select a situation where the consequences of a poor decision were less negative for you. Then employ the same steps that I have outlined above. Work in this way with modified unhealthy regret-related 'A's' until you find your original one 'challenging, but not overwhelming' and then use the steps again.

Step 9: Forgive yourself and show yourself compassion

Even if your unhealthy regret[4] is based on a rigid attitude and an awfulising or an unbearability attitude, it is likely that you will also be critical and unforgiving of yourself for not making the 'right' decision in the relevant circumstances. Thus, it is important that you develop an attitude of self-forgiveness and then develop self-compassion. Here are examples of each in retrospective regret.

Self-forgiveness

⊙ 'I may have made the wrong decision and, if I did, I forgive myself as a fallible human being who did the wrong thing. I am not stupid or an idiot. I am the same person even if I made the right decision. The rightness or wrongness of my decision varies, but I do not.'

Self-compassion

⊙ 'It is difficult being human when there are so many variables to consider before making an important decision. I am not alone in finding it a struggle. The vast majority of people also struggle with this. So, I am going to remind myself that, as I did not set out to make a wrong decision, I am going to give myself a break and recognise that I did the best that I could at the time. Then I will let any remaining self-critical thoughts stay in my mind without engaging with them or trying to get rid of them. They will go as I get on with the business of living.'

Step 10: Capitalise on what you have learned

When you have faced a situation in which you experienced unhealthy regret and dealt with it as best you could, it is important that you reflect on what you did and what you learned. In particular, if you were able to face the situation (in unhealthy regret, this will largely be in your mind), and rehearse your specific flexible/non-extreme attitudes until you felt healthy regret, then ask yourself how you can capitalise on what you achieved. If you experienced any problems, respond to the following questions:

- Did I face the situation and, if not, why not?

- Did I rehearse my flexible/non-extreme attitudes before, during or after facing the situation and, if not, why not?

- Did I execute my plan to face the situation and, if not, why not?

- Did I engage with post-rigid/extreme attitude distorted thinking and, if so, why?

Reflect on your experience and put into practice what you have learned the next time you face a situation in which you consider that you acted in a way you wished you had not acted or failed to act in a way you wished you had acted.

Step 11: Generalise your learning

Once you have dealt with your unhealthy regret in a specific situation by holding the relevant specific version of your general flexible/non-extreme attitude and by acting and thinking in ways that are consistent with it, you can generalise this learning to situations defined by your particular regret-based theme (taking action in the past and wishing you had not done so, failing to take action in the past and wishing you had done so or the uncertainty you face about making a decision now or in the future).

Mary was particularly prone to unhealthy prospective regret about making important life decisions, so she followed the steps outlined in this chapter. Thus:

- Mary assessed the three components of her unhealthy regret response and set goals with respect to all three components.

- She identified her relevant general rigid/extreme attitude regarding making important life decisions (i.e., 'I must be certain that I am doing the right thing and that I will not regret my decision later and I can't bear not having such certainty') that underpinned her unhealthy prospective regret response and her alternative general flexible/non-extreme attitude (i.e., 'I would like to be certain that I am doing the right thing and that I will not regret my decision later, but I don't need such certainty and I can bear not having it') that underpinned her healthy prospective regret response.

- She examined both elements of her general rigid/extreme attitude and her general flexible/non-extreme attitude until she clearly saw that the former were false, made no sense and were detrimental to her, and that the latter were true, sensible and healthy.

- She then recognised that she needed to take action now rather than postponing it and decided to take the job she was offered rather than remain in her current job. When she thought that she was making the wrong decision, she reminded herself that she did not know this and did not need to know it and that she would respond productively to whatever happened in the future. As she did so, she tolerated the discomfort that she felt and accepted that some of her distorted and skewed negative thinking would still be in her mind as she did so. She let such thinking be without engaging with it, suppressing it or distracting herself from it.

As this section shows, you can generalise what you learn about dealing with unhealthy regret from situation to situation as defined by your particular regret-based theme (i.e., taking action in the past and wishing you had not done so, failing to take action in the past and wishing you had done so or facing the uncertainty about making a decision now or in the future). If you do this, you will take the toxicity out of the emotional problem of unhealthy regret!

USING REBT'S ABCD FORM TO DEAL WITH SPECIFIC EXAMPLES OF YOUR UNHEALTHY REGRET

This chapter is mainly geared to help you deal with your unhealthy regret in general terms. However, you can also use this material to address specific examples of your unhealthy regret. I have developed a self-help form to provide the structure to assist you in this regard. It is called the ABCD form and it appears with instructions in Appendix 6.

OTHER IMPORTANT ISSUES IN DEALING WITH UNHEALTHY REGRET

In the above section, I outlined an 11-step programme to deal with unhealthy regret. In this section, I discuss some other important issues that may be relevant to you in your work to become less prone to this emotional problem. If you want to, you can incorporate them as additional steps in the above step-by-step guide at points relevant to you.

Dealing with your safety-seeking measures to avoid unhealthy regret

I mentioned in Chapter 2 that people use safety-seeking measures to protect themselves from threat. You may use similar measures to protect yourself from feeling unhealthy regret. Here is how this works from your perspective. In outlining this, I will use unhealthy prospective regret as an example. You reason that, since you feel unhealthy prospective regret facing the uncertainty about making a decision now or in the future, you will take steps to avoid unhealthy regret by not making a decision until you know for certain that it will have a good outcome for you as your life pans out. Taking this tack means that you will not take risks in life in case you choose a course of action that may turn out badly.

However, this behaviour and the reasoning that leads you to take it are flawed and will serve only to perpetuate your chronic unhealthy regret. This is due to the fact that your unhealthy prospective regret is based, not on you facing the uncertainty about making a decision now or in the future, but on your rigid/extreme attitudes towards this inference. So, if you want to deal effectively with unhealthy regret, you need to take a healthy risk by making a considered decision about a desired course of action without seeking reassurance from others that you are doing the right thing.

Accepting a range of outcomes from making a decision

In 1983, I decided to take voluntary redundancy from my lecturing job at the University of Aston in Birmingham. After two years of applying for jobs, I got a lectureship at Goldsmiths College, where I stayed until I retired in 2014. Did I make the right decision? I don't know is the honest answer because I have no way of determining what would have happened to me if I had stayed at Aston. I may have had a better life, a worse life or it may have made no difference. This is the point. If you have a problem with unhealthy retrospective regret, for example, you tend to think that, if you had made a different decision, it would have turned out better for you. This conclusion is produced by your rigid/extreme attitude towards taking action in the past and wishing you had not done so or failing to take action in the past and wishing you had done so. Once you have developed a flexible/non-extreme attitude towards these inferences, you will see that, when you make a decision and it turns out badly for you, it may be that, if you had decided to do something different, it may have turned out better for you, it may have turned out worse or it may have made no difference.

Accepting that you can't know what you don't know

In unhealthy regret, you tend to hold the view that it is possible to make a decision where everything turns out as you want it to. If it doesn't, then it is your fault, and you warrant self-criticism. However, in reality, all you can do is take action or choose not to take action based on the information available at the time. It is always possible to do more research, but, if you do so, you may delay taking action, which may be a mistake. The idea, then, that you should have known what you did not know, which is prevalent in unhealthy regret, is rigid and preposterous. How can you know what you do not know? Giving up such a demand is central to dealing productively with unhealthy regret.

Why you feel unhealthy regret much of the time and how to deal with this

If you are particularly prone to unhealthy regret, you will often think that you (a) have taken action in the past and wished you had not done so, (b) have failed to take action in the past and wished you had done so or (c) are facing the uncertainty about making a decision now or in the future. You do this because you hold what I call a 'chronic unhealthy regret-based general rigid/extreme attitude'. Here is an example of such an attitude in unhealthy prospective regret.

- 'Whenever I have an important decision to make, I must make sure that it will turn out well. If it doesn't, then it is terrible, I can't bear it and I am a stupid person for not making a better decision.'

You then take this attitude to relevant situations and, when some negative consequences occur when you choose a course of action or fail to take action, you think that you are at fault if there is a bad outcome. As a result, you constantly think that you are responsible for any negative outcomes that happen or might happen and end up criticising yourself.

How to deal with chronic unhealthy regret

In order to deal with this chronic sense of unhealthy regret, you need to develop and apply an alternative general flexible/non-extreme attitude that protects you from such unhealthy regret. Here is an example of such an attitude in healthy prospective regret.

- Whenever I have an important decision to make, I want to make sure that it will turn out well, but I do not have to succeed at this. If it doesn't turn out well, then it is bad, but not terrible, I can bear it and I am not a stupid person for not making a better decision. I am fallible, that's all.'

Such an attitude will lead you to think that you have made a wrong decision only when there is clear evidence for making such an inference. When there is, you will feel healthy regret rather than unhealthy regret because you will be processing this with a specific flexible/non-extreme attitude.

How to examine the accuracy of your unhealthy regret-related inference, if necessary

If you are still unsure if you decided on the wrong course of action in the past, for example, answer one or more of the following questions:

- How valid is my inference that I took the wrong course of action (for example)?

- Would an objective jury agree that I took the wrong course of action? If not, what would the jury's verdict be?

- Is my inference that I took the wrong course of action realistic? If not, what is a more realistic inference?

- If I asked someone whom I could trust to give me an objective opinion about my inference that I took the wrong course of action, what would the person say to me and why? What inference would this person encourage me to make instead?

- If a friend had told me that they had made the same inference about taking the wrong course of action in the same situation, what would I say to them about the validity of their inference and why? What inference would I encourage this friend to make instead?

Identifying and dealing with the hidden conceit in unhealthy regret

It may sound strange, but when you think about unhealthy regret from a particular perspective, an attitude of hidden conceit is revealed. Such conceit is revealed when you are asked to judge someone who has acted in a situation in the same way as you. Let me give an example from unhealthy retrospective regret to make this clear.

> Nathan felt unhealthy retrospective regret whenever he thought about his decision to break off his relationship with his fiancée two years ago. He thought he made a mistake because he is still single while his ex-fiancée is herself engaged. Nathan's rigid/extreme attitude with respect to this decision was: 'I made the wrong decision by breaking off my engagement, and I absolutely should not have done so.' At the same time, Nathan's friend Pete also broke off his engagement and is also still single. When Pete talked about the fact that he also made a mistake, Nathan told him that, if it was a mistake, he is human for doing so and he should cut himself some slack. This was precisely the attitude that Nathan did not apply to himself. He refused to cut himself some slack and regarded himself as stupid for making the mistake that he holds now that he absolutely should not have made. Nathan's hidden conceit is thus revealed in his differential expectations of himself and Pete. He sees Pete as fallible with limitations. He sees himself as someone who must not make the same mistake as he permits Pete to have made. This 'holier than thou' attitude is common in unhealthy regret: 'I must make perfect decisions and, if not, I am stupid.'

It is very important that you deal with this hidden conceit if you want to become less prone to unhealthy regret. You do this in ways that should now be familiar to you:

- By all means have high standards for yourself in making important decisions, but remind yourself that you don't always have to achieve these standards.

- Accept yourself as a fallible human being with limitations in the same way as you would others. Then develop self-compassion. I recommend the writings of Paul Gilbert (e.g., 2009) on this subject.

Assessing and dealing with emotional problems about unhealthy regret

In previous chapters, I discussed the concept of meta-disturbance (literally disturbance about disturbance). It is important to assess carefully the nature of this meta-disturbance about unhealthy regret before you can best deal with it.

The best way to start dealing with the assessment of any emotional problems you might have about unhealthy regret is to ask yourself the question: 'How do I feel about my feeling of unhealthy regret?' The most common emotional problems that people have about unhealthy regret are as follows: anxiety, depression, unhealthy regret, shame and unhealthy self-anger. I refer you to the chapters on anxiety, depression, shame and unhealthy anger for help on how to deal with these meta-emotional problems about unhealthy regret.

Developing and rehearsing healthy regret-based world views

People develop views of the world as it relates to them that makes it more or less likely that they will experience UNEs. The world views that render you vulnerable to unhealthy regret do so in a similar way to the chronic unhealthy regret-based general rigid/extreme attitude discussed above (i.e., 'Whenever I have an important decision to make, I must make sure that it will turn out well. If it doesn't, then it is terrible, I can't bear it and I am a stupid person for not making a better decision) by making you focus unduly on courses of action that you think were wrong, for example. However, these unhealthy regret-based world views have this effect on you much more widely.

It is important that you develop realistic views of the world that will help you to deal with unhealthy regret and experience healthy regret instead. In Table 5.1, you will find an illustrative list of such world views rather than an exhaustive one, so you can get an idea of what I mean, which will enable you to develop your own. In Table 5.1, I first describe a world view that renders you vulnerable to unhealthy regret and then I give its healthy

Table 5.1 World views that render you vulnerable to unhealthy regret and help you to deal with unhealthy regret

Views of the world that render you vulnerable to unhealthy regret	Views of the world that help you deal with unhealthy regret
◉ It is possible to make perfect decisions that have only positive short-term and long-term consequences	◉ It may occasionally be possible to make perfect decisions that have only positive short-term and long-term consequences, but most of the time it's not
◉ As it is possible to make perfect decisions, I must be able to make such decisions and I am stupid if I can't	◉ Even if it is possible to make perfect decisions, it does not follow that I have to do so. If I don't, I'm fallible, not stupid
◉ Unless I have all the relevant information to hand, I must not make important decisions. I can only make such decisions when I am confident that I have all such information at my disposal	◉ It's not always possible to have all the relevant information to hand. If not, I can still decide on a course of action given the information that I have
◉ I need to be certain that I am doing the right thing now and in the future before I make an important decision. It is possible to always act morally	◉ Having certainty that I am doing the right thing now and in the future would be nice, but, as I have only probability to rely on, I will make decisions on the basis of probability, not certainty
◉ If I think long enough, I will discover what I should have done in the past and what I should do now	◉ A certain amount of thinking is good, but too much thinking will lead to pointless rumination. Continuing to think when thinking has not revealed the answer is like digging myself ever deeper into a hole

alternative. You will see that the latter views are characterised by the idea that you are fallible and can make good and bad decisions, whereas, in the former, you must only make good decisions.

If you hold flexible/non-extreme attitudes that are consistent with the views of the world listed on the right-hand side of Table 5.1, and if you act and think in ways that are, in turn, consistent with these flexible/non-extreme attitudes, you will become less prone to unhealthy regret.

In Chapter 6, I discuss shame and how to deal with it.

NOTES

1 Such a decision may involve choosing a course of action or choosing not to act.
2 By 'best decision' here, I mean a course of action (or inaction) that would have resulted in a situation where the person would have no regrets about what they did or did not do.
3 Whether or not you made a wrong decision is a question for later. In REBT, in order for you to deal effectively with your unhealthy regret, it is important for you to assume *temporarily* that you did make the wrong decision.
4 While this section is particularly relevant in unhealthy retrospective regret, it also applies to unhealthy prospective regret. However, I will focus on the former here.

6

Dealing with shame

In this chapter, I begin by presenting REBT's way of understanding shame and then address how to deal with this emotional problem.

UNDERSTANDING SHAME

In understanding shame, we need to know what we tend to make ourselves feel ashamed about (i.e., its major inference themes), what attitudes we hold, how we act or tend to act, and how we think when we feel ashamed. While shame and guilt are often seen as similar emotions (and they both involve self-devaluation), they differ in the following respects:

⊚ The inference themes are different, as we shall see.

⊚ In guilt, you tend only to devalue yourself about your own behaviour and its consequences, while you can feel ashamed not only about your own behaviour, but also about the behaviour of members of a social group with whom you closely identify. Thus, while you may talk about bringing shame on your family, you tend not to talk about bringing guilt on your family.

⊚ You tend to act and think in different ways when you feel shame than when you feel guilt.

Major inference themes in shame

There are three major themes in relation to your personal domain that are implicated in shame:

⊚ Something highly negative has been revealed about you (or about a group with whom you identify) by yourself or by others.

⊚ You have acted in a way that falls very short of your ideal.

DOI: 10.4324/9781003424307-6

◉ Others look down on or shun you (or a group with whom you identify) or you think that they do.

Rigid/extreme attitudes

As I explained in Chapter 1, according to REBT, inferences on their own do not account for emotional problems. It is possible, therefore, for you to make the same inferences as listed above and be disappointed, but not ashamed.[1] In order for you to feel ashamed when you think that (a) something highly negative has been revealed about you (or about a group with whom you identify) by yourself or by others, (b) you have acted in a way that falls very short of your ideal and/or (c) others look down on or shun you (or a group with whom you identify) or you think that they do, you have to hold a rigid/extreme attitude. As with guilt (see Chapter 4), in shame you hold a rigid attitude and an extreme self-devaluation attitude.

Behaviour associated with shame

When you hold a rigid/extreme attitude towards(a) something highly negative being revealed about you (or about a group with whom you identify) by yourself or by others, (b) acting in a way that falls very short of your ideal and/or (c) others looking down on or shunning you (or a group with whom you identify), you will act or tend to act in a number of ways, the most common of which are as follows:

◉ You remove yourself from the 'gaze' of others.

◉ You isolate yourself from others.

◉ You save face by attacking other(s) who have 'shamed' you.

◉ You defend your threatened self-esteem in self-defeating ways.

◉ You ignore attempts by others to restore social equilibrium.

Thinking associated with shame

When you hold a rigid/extreme attitude towards(a) something highly negative being revealed about you (or a group with whom you identify) by yourself or by others, (b) acting in a way that falls very short of your ideal and/or (c) others looking down on or shunning you (or a group with whom you identify), you will tend to think in a number of ways. Remember what I said in Chapter 1: the thinking that accompanies your shame is the result of your shame-based inference being processed by your rigid/extreme attitude and therefore it is likely to contain a number of thinking errors that I present in Appendix 1. I list the main features of this post-rigid/extreme attitude shame-based thinking below:

- You overestimate the negativity of the information revealed.

- You overestimate the likelihood that the judging group will notice or be interested in the information.

- You overestimate the degree of disapproval you (or your reference group) will receive.

- You overestimate how long any disapproval will last.

As you can see, such thinking exaggerates the negative social consequences of your behaviour (or that of the member of your identified social group) and also ignores the role of context. Such thinking may be in words or in mental images.

HOW TO DEAL WITH SHAME

If you are prone to shame, you tend to experience this emotional problem in a variety of different settings and in response to a variety of situations where something highly negative has been revealed about you (or about a group with whom you identify) by yourself or by others; you have acted in a way that falls very short of your ideal and/or others look down on or shun you (or a group with whom you identify) or you think that they do. Here is how to deal with shame so that you become less prone to it.

Step 1: Identify reasons why shame is a problem for you and why you want to change

While shame is generally regarded as an emotional problem, it is useful for you to spell out reasons why shame is a problem for you and why you want to change. I suggest that you keep a written list of these reasons and refer to it as needed as a reminder of why you are engaged in a self-help programme. I discuss the healthy alternative to shame in Step 4.

Step 2: Take responsibility for your shame

In REBT, we argue that what you do or what people think of you do not make you feel ashamed; rather you create these feelings by the rigid/ extreme attitudes that you hold towards what you do and what people think of you. Unless you accept this point, you will not address your shame productively. Rather, you will think that the only way not to feel ashamed is by always achieving the ideal standards that you have for yourself or ensuring that others think well of you. This view will perpetuate your shame rather than help you deal with it.

Step 3: Identify the themes you tend to be ashamed about

The best way of identifying shame-related inference themes to which you are particularly vulnerable is by understanding the themes associated with shame, and seeing which are present when you feel ashamed. As I outlined above, there are three such themes:

- Something highly negative has been revealed about you (or about a group with whom you identify) by yourself or by others.
- You have acted in a way that falls very short of your ideal.
- Others look down on or shun you (or a group with whom you identify) or you think that they do.

Step 4: Identify the three components of your shame response and set goals with respect to each component

The next step is for you to list the three elements of your shame response in the face of each of the relevant themes listed above.

Identify the three components of your shame response

I use the term 'shame response' to describe the three main components that make up this response. The three components of your shame response are the emotional, behavioural and thinking components.

Emotional component

The emotional component here is, of course, shame.

Behavioural component

The behavioural component concerns overt behaviour or action tendencies that you engage in or 'feel like' engaging in when you feel shame. Consult the list that I provided to help you identify your behaviour associated with each relevant theme when you feel shame (see p. 107).

Thinking component

The thinking component associated with shame is listed on p. 108. Again, these may be in words or in mental pictures. Consult this list if necessary.

Set goals with respect to each of the three components

You need to set goals so that you know what you are striving for when you deal effectively with shame. The three goals are emotional, behavioural and thinking goals.

Emotional goal

Your emotional goal is disappointment rather than shame (or whatever synonym you prefer to the term 'disappointment'). Disappointment is an HNE, which is an appropriate response to the three shame-related themes detailed above. It helps you to think objectively about the situation and your response to it and helps you to move on with your life rather than get stuck or bogged down.

Behavioural goal

Your behavioural goal should reflect actions that are based on disappointment rather than shame. The following are the most common behaviours associated with disappointment. You may wish to compare these behaviours with those associated with shame that I presented on p. 107.

- You continue to participate actively in social interaction.
- You respond positively to attempts of others to restore social equilibrium.

Thinking goal

As well as setting behavioural goals related to the feeling of disappointment about (a) something highly negative being revealed about you (or about a group with whom you identify) by yourself or by others, (b) acting in a way that falls very short of your ideal and/or (c) others looking down on or shunning you (or a group with whom you identify), it is important that you set thinking goals associated with this emotion. The following are the most common forms of thinking associated with disappointment rather than shame. Again, you may wish to compare these forms of thinking with those associated with shame that I presented on p. 108.

- You see the information revealed in a compassionate self-accepting context.

- You are realistic about the likelihood that the judging group will notice or be interested in the information revealed.

- You are realistic about the degree of disapproval self (or reference group) will receive.

- You are realistic about how long any disapproval will last.

As the above list shows, the dominant feature of thinking associated with disappointment is that it is realistic and balanced. Please remember that such thinking may be in words or in mental pictures.

Step 5: Identify your general rigid/extreme attitudes and alternative general flexible/non-extreme attitudes

A general rigid/extreme attitude leading to your shame response is a rigid/extreme attitude that you hold across situations defined by one of the following themes:

- Something highly negative has been revealed about you (or about a group with whom you identify) by yourself or by others.

- You have acted in a way that falls very short of your ideal.

- Others look down on or shun you (or a group with whom you identify) or you think that they do.

Its flexible/non-extreme alternative, which will also be general in nature, will account for your disappointment response.

Identify your general rigid/extreme attitudes

When you identify a general rigid/extreme attitude, you take a common shame-related theme (see above) and add to this a general rigid attitude and the main extreme attitude that is derived from the rigid attitude. In shame, your main extreme attitude will be a self-devaluation attitude. For example:

⊙ 'I must not fall short of my high social standards and I am defective if I do.'

Identify your alternative general flexible/non-extreme attitudes

When you identify your alternative general flexible/non-extreme attitude, you take the same common theme – (a) something highly negative has been revealed about you (or about a group with whom you identify) by yourself or by others, (b) you have acted in a way that falls very short of your ideal or (c) others look down on or shun you (or a group with whom you identify) or you think that they do – and add to this a general flexible attitude and a general unconditional self-acceptance attitude. For example:

⊙ 'I really don't want to fall very short of my high social standards, but that does not mean that I must not do so. If I do it would be unfortunate, but it would not prove that I am defective. Rather it proves that I am fallible.'

Step 6: Examine your general attitudes

I recommended in previous chapters that you first examine together your general rigid attitude and its general flexible attitude alternative and then examine together your general extreme attitude and your general non-extreme attitude.

Examine your general rigid attitude and its general flexible attitude alternative

First, take your general rigid attitude and its general flexible attitude alternative and write them down next to one another on a sheet of paper. Then ask yourself:

⊙ Which is true and which is false?

⊙ Which is sensible logically and which does not make sense?

⊙ Which has largely constructive results and which has largely unconstructive results?

Write down your answer to each of these questions on your piece of paper, giving reasons for each answer. Consult Appendix 2 for help with the answers to these questions, which you need to adapt and apply to the attitudes you are examining.

Examine your general self-devaluation attitude and its general unconditional self-acceptance attitude alternative

Next, take your general self-devaluation attitude and its general unconditional self-acceptance attitude alternative and again write them down next to one another on a sheet of paper. Then, ask yourself the same three questions that you used with your general rigid attitude and its general flexible attitude alternative. Again, write down your answer to each of these questions on your piece of paper, giving reasons for each answer. I suggest that you consult Appendix 5 (for help with examining self-devaluation attitudes and unconditional self-acceptance attitudes). Again, you need to adapt and apply these arguments to the attitudes you are examining.

   You should now be ready to commit to acting and thinking in ways consistent with your general flexible/non-extreme attitude.

Step 7: Adopt a healthy orientation towards your high standards

Once you have committed yourself to strengthening your conviction in your general flexible/non-extreme attitude, it is useful for you to develop what I call a healthy orientation towards your high standards. This involves you doing the following:

- Recognise that there is nothing intrinsically wrong with having high standards.

- View these standards as signposts to aim for rather than as yardsticks that you must achieve. As such, your high standards are similar to self-actualisation in that you can never achieve them once and for all. Rather you can work steadily to achieve them.

- Accept that, when you fail to live up to your high standards, the best way of dealing with this situation is to learn from it and to apply your learning on future occasions having first accepted yourself unconditionally for your failure.

Step 8: Face your shame-related theme in imagery

I hope that you have made a commitment to act on your general flexible/non-extreme attitudes (i.e., flexible attitude and unconditional self-acceptance attitude). Assuming that you have, your basic task is face up to (a) something highly negative being revealed about you (or about a group with whom you identify) by yourself or by others, (b) acting in a way that falls very short of your ideal and/or (c) others looking down on or shunning you (or a group with whom you identify) or you think that they do and to learn to think in flexible/non-extreme ways about it.

Up to this point, you have worked at a general level with respect to your shame-related theme, dealing with the general rigid/extreme attitudes that account for your shame and developing your alternative general flexible/non-extreme attitudes. However, when you come to apply your general flexible/non-extreme attitudes in dealing with shame-related themes, you need to bear in mind one important point. Since you make yourself ashamed about specific events (actual or imagined), you need to deal with these by rehearsing specific variants of your general flexible/non-extreme attitudes.

While the best way to do this is in specific shame-related situations, you may derive benefit by using imagery first. If this is the case, you need to do the following:

- Imagine a specific situation in which you felt shame or may feel shame about (a) something highly negative being revealed about you (or about a group with whom you identify) by yourself or by others, (b) acting in a way that falls very short of your ideal or (c) others looking down on or shunning you (or a group with whom you identify) or you think that they do and focus, in your mind's eye, on what you felt most ashamed about (i.e., your 'A').

- Focus on this 'A' while rehearsing a specific flexible/non-extreme attitude relevant to the situation. As you do this, try to make yourself feel disappointed, rather than ashamed.

- Then see yourself acting in ways consistent with your flexible/non-extreme attitude, e.g., holding your head up high and admitting publicly to any pratfalls.

- Recognise that some of your post-rigid/extreme-attitude thinking may be distorted. Respond to it without getting bogged down doing so. Accept the presence of any remaining distorted thoughts without engaging with them.

- Repeat the above steps until you feel sufficiently ready to put this sequence into practice in your life.

If you find that facing your shame-related 'A', in your mind's eye, is too much for you, use the 'challenging, but not overwhelming' principle that I introduced in Chapter 2 (see p. 33). This means that, instead of imagining yourself facing a shame-related situation that you find 'overwhelming' at the present time, choose a similar shame-related 'A' that you would find 'challenging, but not overwhelming'. Then employ the same steps that I have outlined above. Work in this way with modified shame-related 'As' until you find your original one 'challenging, but not overwhelming' and then use the steps again.

Step 9: Face situations and people with your head held high

Having learned the lessons from previous shame-based episodes, you are ready to go back to the social milieu and hold your head up as you do so.

- Choose a specific situation in which you will be reminded of your 'fall from grace' and about which you would ordinarily feel ashamed.

- Rehearse a specific version of your general flexible/non-extreme attitudes before entering the situation so that you can be prepared to face the music while in a flexible/non-extreme frame of mind.

- Develop a shortened version of this flexible/non-extreme attitude in mind as you enter the situation (e.g., 'I'm still fallible even though I have fallen from grace') and accept the fact that you are likely to be uncomfortable while doing so. React to any consequences from a flexible/non-extreme frame of mind if you can.

- Recognise that, even though you have got yourself into a flexible/non-extreme frame of mind, some of your thinking may be distorted and unrealistic and some may be realistic and balanced. Accept the presence of the former and do not engage with it. Engage with the latter as much as you can.

Step 10: Capitalise on what you have learned

When you have faced a situation in which you experienced shame and dealt with it as best you could, it is important that you reflect on what you did and what you learned. In particular, if you were able to face the situation, and rehearse your specific flexible/non-extreme attitudes until you felt disappointment, then ask yourself how you can capitalise on what you achieved. If you experienced any problems, respond to the following questions:

- Did I face the situation and, if not, why not?

- Did I rehearse my flexible/non-extreme attitudes before, during or after facing the situation and, if not, why not?

- Did I execute my plan to face the situation and, if not, why not?

- Did I engage with post-rigid/extreme attitude distorted thinking and, if so, why?

Reflect on your experience and put into practice what you have learned the next time you face a situation in which (a) something highly negative was revealed about you (or about a group with whom you identify) by yourself or by others, (b) you acted in a way that falls very short of your ideal or (c) others looked down on or shunned you (or a group with whom you identify) or you think that they did.

Step 11: Generalise your learning

Once you have dealt with your shame in a specific situation by holding the relevant specific version of your general flexible/non-extreme attitude and by acting and thinking in ways that are consistent with it, you can generalise this learning to situations defined by your shame-based theme.

Miranda was particularly prone to shame about falling very short of her ideal of acting with decorum. Thus:

- Miranda assessed the three components of her shame response and set goals with respect to all three components.

- She identified her relevant general rigid/extreme attitude regarding falling very short of her standards (i.e., 'I must achieve my high behavioural standards and I am a disgrace if I don't') that underpinned her shame response and her alternative general flexible/non-extreme attitude (i.e., 'I want to achieve my high behavioural standards, but I don't always have to do so. If I do not achieve my high standards, it is bad, but I am not a disgrace. I am an ordinary fallible person who has done something unfortunate') that underpinned her disappointment response.

- She examined both elements of her general rigid/extreme attitude and her general flexible/non-extreme attitude until she clearly saw that the former were false, made no sense and were detrimental to her, and that the latter were true, sensible and healthy.

- She acted on her flexible/non-extreme attitudes in specific situations, held her head up and engaged in eye contact as she did so, even though people tended to look down on her.

- As she did so, she tolerated the discomfort that she felt and accepted that some of her distorted and skewed negative thinking would still be in her mind. She let such thinking be without engaging with it, suppressing it or distracting herself from it.

As this section shows, you can generalise what you learn about dealing with shame from situation to situation as defined by your shame-based inference.

USING REBT'S ABCD FORM TO DEAL WITH SPECIFIC EXAMPLES OF YOUR SHAME

This chapter is mainly geared to help you deal with your shame in general terms. However, you can also use this material to address specific examples of your shame. I have developed a self-help form to provide the structure to assist you in this regard. It is called the ABCD form and it appears with instructions in Appendix 6.

OTHER IMPORTANT ISSUES IN DEALING WITH SHAME

In the above section, I outlined an 11-step programme to deal with shame. In this section, I discuss some other important issues that may be relevant to you in your work to become less prone to this emotional problem. If you want to, you can incorporate them as additional steps in the above step-by-step guide at points relevant to you.

Dealing with your safety-seeking measures to avoid shame

I mentioned in Chapter 2 that people use safety-seeking measures to protect themselves from threat. You may use similar measures to protect yourself from feeling shame. Here is how this works from your perspective. You reason that, since you feel ashamed about (a) something highly negative being revealed about you (or about a group with whom you identify) by yourself or by others, (b) acting in a way that falls very short of your ideal and/or (c) others looking down on or shunning you (or a group with whom you identify), you will take two major steps to avoid shame. First, you will always act in ways that are socially acceptable and get those with whom you are connected to do the same thing as well. Second, you will avoid situations where you may fall very short of your ideal. Taking this decision means that you will not take risks in life (in case you do socially unacceptable things or fall very short of your ideal) and you will curtail the autonomy of others in case they 'shame' you.

However, this behaviour and the reasoning that leads you to take it are flawed and will serve only to perpetuate your chronic shame. This is due

to the fact that your shame is not based on (a) something highly negative being revealed about you (or about a group with whom you identify)
by yourself or by others, (b) acting in a way that falls very short of your
ideal and/or (c) others looking down on or shunning you (or a group with
whom you identify), but on your rigid/extreme attitudes towards these
three inferences. So, if you want to deal effectively with shame, you need
to do the following:

- Take healthy risks and let others with whom you are connected do
  the same and see what happens. You will probably find that people
  do not disapprove as much as you think and that, while you may fall
  short of your ideal, this fall from grace will not be as dramatic as you
  predicted.

- However, if as a result of your behaviour or that of others, something
  highly negative is revealed, you do fall very short of your ideal or that
  others do highly disapprove or shun you (or others with whom you are
  connected), then you can deal with such situations by holding a set of
  flexible/non-extreme attitudes towards them so that you feel healthy
  disappointment and not shame about these consequences.

Why you feel shame much of the time and how to deal with this

If you are particularly prone to shame, you will often focus on times where
(a) something highly negative has been revealed about you (or about a
group with whom you identify) by yourself or by others, (b) you have
acted in a way that falls very short of your ideal and (c) others look down
on or shun you (or a group with whom you identify) or you think that
they do. You do this because you hold the following attitude, which I call
a 'chronic shame-based general rigid/extreme attitude':

- I must ensure that I and people with whom I am closely connected must
  always achieve the highest of standards and be socially approved and, if
  not, it proves that we are defective, disgusting or diminished.'

You then take this attitude to situations where it is possible that you and
others will fall short or be socially disapproved of, and you attempt to
protect all involved from the predicted negative outcomes by getting all

to maintain standards or withdraw so that social approval is maintained. However, in doing so, you are keeping alive the three inferences of shame. For you are saying to yourself that, if I did not take the appropriate steps, the following would have happened:

- Something highly negative would be revealed about you (or about a group with whom you identify) by yourself or by others.

- You would act in a way that falls very short of your ideal.

- Others would look down on or shun you (or a group with whom you identify).

How to deal with chronic shame

In order to deal with this chronic sense of shame, you need to develop and apply an alternative general flexible/non-extreme attitude that protects you from such shame:

- 'I would like to ensure that I and people with whom I am closely connected always achieve the highest standards and are socially approved, but I do not have to do so. If I do not it would be unfortunate, but it would not prove that we are defective, disgusting or diminished. Rather, it would prove that we are fallible human beings and that does not change whether or not we fall from grace and are disapproved of.'

Such an attitude will lead you to think that the following occurred only when there is clear evidence for making such an inference:

- Something highly negative has been revealed about you (or about a group with whom you identify) by yourself or by others.

- You have acted in a way that falls very short of your ideal.

- Others look down on or shun you (or a group with whom you identify) or you think that they do.

When there is such evidence, you will feel disappointment rather than shame because you will be processing this with a specific flexible/non-extreme attitude.

How to examine the accuracy of your shame-related inference, if necessary

If you are still unsure whether (a) something highly negative has been revealed about you (or about a group with whom you identify) by yourself or by others, (b) you have acted in a way that falls very short of your ideal or (c) others looked down on or shunned you (or a group with whom you identify), answer one or more of the following questions:

- How valid is my inference that I have fallen very short of my ideal (for example)?

- Would an objective jury agree that I have fallen very short of my ideal? If not, what would the jury's verdict be?

- Is my inference that I have fallen very short of my ideal realistic? If not, what is a more realistic inference?

- If I asked someone whom I could trust to give me an objective opinion about my inference that I have fallen very short of my ideal, what would the person say to me and why? What inference would this person encourage me to make instead?

- If a friend had told me that they had made the same inference about falling very short of their ideal in the same situation, what would I say to them about the validity of their inference and why? What inference would I encourage the person to make instead?

The Individual 'I' and the Socially Defined 'I'

If you have a problem with shame, you probably find it difficult to conceive that you can hold an attitude towards yourself (i.e., the Individual 'I') that is radically different from how others see you (i.e., the Socially Defined 'I'). Yet this is your task if it does transpire that people consider you defective, disgusting or diminished either for falling very short of your ideal or for acting in a way that is greatly at variance from the mores of the judging social group.

In REBT, we argue that it is possible for you to accept yourself as a fallible human being in the face of others considering you defective, disgusting or diminished. Let me show you how Shireen used a technique that I call Dryden's Invitation Technique.

Shireen came from a close-knit religious Muslim family, but was not religious herself. When she went to college, she met and fell in love with a young Hindu man. When her family and community discovered this, they put her under enormous pressure to end the relationship, which she refused to do. Then they told her that, because she was defective, they did not want to have anything to do with her. Initially, Shireen felt intense shame when they told her that she was defective. Then, she helped herself by using Dryden's Invitation Technique in the following way:

- Shireen recognised that, when her family considered her defective, they were in fact issuing her with an invitation, saying in effect: 'We regard you as defective for going against your family and social group and we invite you to define yourself as defective.'

- Shireen then recognised that, as with a wedding invitation, she had a choice to accept or decline the invitation. Thus, she could say:

  - 'Thank you for your invitation for me to agree with you. I accept' or

  - 'Thank you for your invitation for me to agree with you. I decline'.

- Shireen chose to decline the invitation and felt disappointed, but not ashamed, about going against her family and social group.

- Had Shireen accepted the invitation, she would have felt ashamed.

As Shireen has shown, it is possible to hold on to a healthy definition of yourself (i.e., the Individual 'I') in the face of others' unhealthy definition of you (i.e., the Socially Defined 'I').

Assessing and dealing with emotional problems about shame

In previous chapters, I discussed the concept of meta-disturbance (literally disturbance about disturbance). It is important to assess carefully the nature of this meta-disturbance about shame before you can best deal with it.

The best way to start dealing with the assessment of any emotional problems you might have about shame is to ask yourself the question: 'How do I feel about my feeling of shame?' The most common emotional problems that people have about shame are as follows: anxiety, depression, unhealthy regret, shame and unhealthy self-anger. I refer you to the chapters on anxiety, depression, unhealthy regret and unhealthy anger for help on how to deal with these meta-emotional problems about shame. Here I will help you to deal with your meta-shame.

Dealing with shame about shame

When you experience shame about shame, you take your original feelings of shame and regard them as evidence of you falling very short of your ideal. Then you hold the following rigid and self-devaluation attitudes towards this 'fall from grace' and experience meta-shame:

● 'I must not fall from grace by experiencing shame and I am defective for so doing.'

First, you need to develop a healthy alternative to these attitudes, such as:

● 'I would much prefer not to fall from grace by experiencing shame, but that doesn't mean that I must not have this feeling. If I do, it's unfortunate, but does not prove I am defective. It proves that I am an ordinary, fallible human being capable of experiencing a range of healthy and unhealthy emotions including shame. Shame does not and cannot define me!'

Examine both sets of attitudes (referring to Appendices 2 and 5 for guidance) and do so until you can fully commit yourself to your flexible/non-extreme attitudes. Then you can openly admit to yourself and to others that you sometimes feel ashamed. In doing so, you are coming out of your shame closet and, as shame hates the light and disclosure to others, you will feel disappointed, not ashamed, by your original shame. When you have done this, you are best placed to deal effectively with this original feeling of shame.

Developing and rehearsing non-shame, disappointment-based world views

People develop views of the world as it relates to them that make it more or less likely that they will experience UNEs. The world views that render you vulnerable to shame do so in a similar way to the chronic shame-based general rigid/extreme attitude discussed above (i.e., 'I must ensure that I and people that I am closely connected with must always achieve the highest standards and be socially approved and, if not, it proves that we are defective, disgusting or diminished'), by making you focus unduly on times when you fell very short of your ideal standards and times when you or others acted against important social mores and by leading you to over-estimate the frequency of such events happening. However, these shame-based world views have this effect on you much more widely.

It is important that you develop realistic views of the world that will help you to deal with shame and experience healthy disappointment instead. In Table 6.1, you will find an illustrative list of such world views rather than an exhaustive one, so you can get an idea of what I mean, which will enable you to develop your own. In Table 6.1, I first describe a world view that renders you vulnerable to shame and then I give its healthy alternative. You will see that the former views are characterised by a conception of the social world as highly dangerous in which, if you slip up, you will be revealed to the harsh judging group as defective, disgusting or diminished.

Table 6.1 World views that render you vulnerable to shame and help you to deal with shame

Views of the world that render you vulnerable to shame	Views of the world that help you deal with shame
◉ There is always the danger that I will not achieve my ideal standards	◉ There is always this danger, but these standards are there to guide me, not to be achieved all the time
◉ Social situations are dangerous because other people will judge me negatively if I put a foot wrong	◉ Social situations can be dangerous, but they can also be benign. If I put a foot wrong, people may judge me negatively, but they may also show me understanding and compassion
◉ Social situations are dangerous because I may be exposed as defective, disgusting or diminished at any moment	◉ If I fall short of my ideal or go against a social custom, I am revealing my fallibility and my humanity. This makes facing social situations far less dangerous

In the latter, a more forgiving picture of others is revealed and a variety of responses to your 'shameful' behaviour can be expected.

If you hold flexible/non-extreme attitudes that are consistent with the views of the world listed on the right-hand side of Table 6.1, and if you act and think in ways that are, in turn, consistent with these flexible/non-extreme attitudes, you will become less prone to shame.

In Chapter 7, I discuss hurt and how to deal with it.

NOTE

1 I regard disappointment as the HNE alternative to shame and I use this term throughout this chapter. However, as we do not have agreed terms for HNEs, feel free to use your own term to denote the healthy alternative to shame.

Dealing with hurt

In this chapter, I begin by presenting REBT's way of understanding hurt and then address how to deal with this emotional problem.

UNDERSTANDING HURT

In understanding hurt, we need to know what we tend to make ourselves feel hurt about (i.e., its major inference themes), what attitudes we hold, how we act or tend to act, and how we think when we feel hurt.

Major inference themes in feeling hurt

There are two major themes in relation to your personal domain that are implicated in feeling hurt:

⊛ Others treat you badly (and you think you do not deserve such treatment).

⊛ You think that the other person has devalued your relationship (i.e., someone indicates that their relationship with you is less important to them than the relationship is to you).

Rigid/extreme attitudes

As I explained in Chapter 1, according to REBT, inferences on their own do not account for emotional problems. It is possible, therefore, for you to make the same inferences as listed above and feel sorrowful and not hurt. In order for you to feel hurt, you have to hold a rigid/extreme attitude. While the rigid attitude is at the core of hurt, the extreme attitudes that are derived from the rigid attitude often distinguish between whether you

DOI: 10.4324/9781003424307-7

are experiencing ego 'less me' hurt (where you devalue yourself) or non-ego 'poor me' hurt (where you 'awfulise', find the adversity unbearable or devalue life).

Behaviour associated with hurt

When you hold a rigid/extreme attitude towards one of the two major inference themes, you will act or tend to act in a number of ways, the most common of which are as follows:

- You stop the communicating channel with the other person.
- You sulk and make it obvious you feel hurt without disclosing details of the matter.
- You indirectly criticise or punish the other person for their offence.

Thinking associated with feeling hurt

When you hold a rigid/extreme attitude towards being unfairly treated by someone close to you, or about another indicating that their relationship to you is less important to them than it is to you, you will tend to think in a number of ways. Remember what I said in Chapter 1: the thinking that accompanies your hurt is the result of your hurt-based inference being processed by your rigid/extreme attitude and therefore it is likely to contain a number of thinking errors that I present in Appendix 1. I list the main features of this post-rigid/extreme attitude hurt-based thinking below:

- You overestimate the unfairness of the other person's behaviour.
- You think that the other person does not care for you or is indifferent to you.
- You see yourself as alone, uncared for or misunderstood.
- You tend to think of past 'hurts'.
- You expect the other to make the first move toward repairing the relationship.

As you can see, such thinking exaggerates the negative consequences of being treated unfairly or having your relationship devalued by others. Such thinking may be in words or in mental images.

HOW TO DEAL WITH FEELING HURT

If you are prone to feeling hurt, you tend to experience this emotional problem in a variety of different settings and in response to a variety of situations where someone thinks less of their relationship with you than you do or where someone treats you badly when you don't deserve it. Here is how to deal with feeling hurt so that you become less prone to it.

Step 1: Identify reasons why feeling hurt is a problem for you and why you want to change

While feeling hurt is generally regarded as an emotional problem, it is useful for you to spell out reasons why feeling hurt is a problem for you and why you want to change. I suggest that you keep a written list of these reasons and refer to it as needed as a reminder of why you are engaged in a self-help programme. I discuss the healthy alternative to feeling hurt in Step 4.

Step 2: Take responsibility for your hurt

In REBT, we argue that people do not hurt you; rather you create these hurt feelings by the rigid/extreme attitudes that you hold towards how people treat you. You may object that this view condones other people's behaviour, but this objection is based on a misconception. You can take responsibility for creating your hurt and still not condone others' bad behaviour.

Step 3: Identify themes you tend to feel hurt about

The best way of identifying hurt-related inference themes to which you are particularly vulnerable is by understanding the themes associated with hurt, and seeing which are present when you feel hurt. As I outlined above, there are two such themes:

- Others treat you badly (and you think you do not deserve such treatment).

- You think that the other person has devalued your relationship (i.e., someone indicates that their relationship with you is less important to them than the relationship is to you).

Step 4: Identify the three components of your hurt response and set goals with respect to each component

The next step is for you to list the three elements of your hurt response in the face of each of the relevant themes listed above.

Identify the three components of your hurt response

I use the term 'hurt response' to describe the three main components that make up this response. The three components of your hurt response are emotional, behavioural and thinking components.

Emotional component

The emotional component here is, of course, hurt.

Behavioural component

The behavioural component concerns overt behaviour or action tendencies that you engage in or 'feel like' engaging in when you feel hurt. Consult the list that I provided to help you identify your behaviour associated with each relevant theme when you feel hurt (see p. 127).

Thinking component

The thinking component associated with hurt is listed on p. 127. Again, these may be in words or in mental pictures. Consult this list if necessary.

Set goals with respect to each of the three components

You need to set goals so that you know what you are striving for when you deal effectively with hurt. The three goals are emotional, behavioural and thinking goals.

Emotional goal

Your emotional goal is sorrow rather than hurt (or whatever synonym you prefer to the term 'sorrow'). Sorrow is an HNE, which is an appropriate response to the two hurt-related themes detailed above. It helps you to think objectively about the situation and your response to it and helps you to move on with your life rather than get stuck or bogged down.

Behavioural goal

Your behavioural goal should reflect actions that are based on sorrow rather than hurt. The following are the most common behaviours associated with sorrow. You may wish to compare these behaviours with those associated with hurt that I presented on p. 127.

- You communicate your feelings to the other directly.

- You request that the other person acts in a fairer manner towards you.

Thinking goal

As well as setting behavioural goals related to the feeling of sorrow about (a) being unfairly treated by someone close to you or about (b) another indicating that their relationship to you is less important to them than it is to you, it is important that you set thinking goals associated with this emotion. The following are the most common forms of thinking associated with sorrow rather than hurt. Again, you may wish to compare these forms of thinking with those associated with hurt that I presented on p. 127.

- You are realistic about the degree of unfairness in the other person's behaviour.

- You think that the other person has acted badly rather than demonstrating lack of caring or indifference.

- You see yourself as being in a poor situation, but still connected to, cared for by and understood by others not directly involved in the situation.

- If you think of past hurts, you do so with less frequency and less intensity than when you feel hurt.

- You are open to the idea of making the first move towards the other person.

As the above list shows, the dominant feature of thinking associated with sorrow is that it is realistic and balanced. Please remember that such thinking may be in words or in mental pictures.

Step 5: Identify your general rigid/extreme attitudes and alternative general flexible/non-extreme attitudes

A general rigid/extreme attitude leading to your hurt response is a rigid/extreme attitude that you hold across situations defined by one of the following themes:

◉ Others treat you badly (and you think you do not deserve such treatment).

◉ Relationship devaluation (i.e., someone indicates that their relationship with you is less important to them than the relationship is to you).

Its flexible/non-extreme alternative, which will also be general in nature, will account for your sorrow response.

Identify your general rigid/extreme attitudes

When you identify a general rigid/extreme attitude, you take a common hurt-related theme (see above) and add to this a general rigid attitude and the main extreme attitude that is derived from the rigid attitude. In hurt, your main extreme attitude will be either an unbearability attitude with an accompanying sense of 'self-pity' (I call this 'poor me' hurt) or a self-devaluation attitude (I call this 'less me' hurt).

Here is an example of each type of hurt:

◉ 'Poor me' hurt:

'I must not be treated unfairly by people close to me when I don't deserve to be and I can't bear it when this happens. Poor me!'

◉ 'Less me' hurt:

'When my relationship with people is important to me, they must find the relationship equally important to them. If they don't, it proves that I am less worthy.'

Identify your alternative general flexible/non-extreme attitudes

When you identify your alternative general flexible/non-extreme attitude, you take the same common theme – i.e., others treat you badly (and you think you do not deserve such treatment) and relationship devaluation (i.e., someone indicates that their relationship with you is less important to them than the relationship is to you) – and add to this a general flexible attitude and a general discomfort tolerance attitude or a general self-acceptance attitude. For example:

- Non-self-pity based sorrow:

  'I don't want to be treated unfairly by people close to me when I don't deserve to be, but they don't have to treat me the way I want them to. When this happens, it is a struggle, but I can stand it and I am not a poor person, even though I have been treated poorly.'

- Unconditional self-acceptance based sorrow:

  'When my relationship with people is important to me, I want them to find the relationship equally important to them, but they don't have to do so. If they don't, it would be bad, but it would not prove that I am less worthy. I am the same person whether or not they value our relationship as much as I do.'

Step 6: Examine your general attitudes

I recommended in previous chapters that you first examine together your general rigid attitude and its general flexible attitude alternative and then examine together your general extreme attitude and its general non-extreme attitude alternative.

Examine your general rigid attitude and its general flexible attitude alternative

First, take your general rigid attitude and its general flexible attitude alternative and write them down next to one another on a sheet of paper. Then ask yourself:

- Which is true and which is false?

- Which is sensible logically and which does not make sense?

- Which has largely constructive results and which has largely unconstructive results?

Write down your answer to each of these questions on your piece of paper, giving reasons for each answer. Consult Appendix 2 for help with the answers to these questions, which you need to adapt and apply to the attitudes you are examining.

Examine your general extreme attitude and its general non-extreme attitude alternative

Next, take your general extreme attitude and its general non-extreme attitude alternative and again write them down next to one another on a sheet of paper. Then, ask yourself the same three questions that you used with your general rigid attitude and its general flexible attitude alternative. Again, write down your answer to each of these questions on your piece of paper, giving reasons for each answer. I suggest that you consult Appendix 3 (for help with examining awfulising attitudes and non-awfulising attitudes), Appendix 4 (for help with examining unbearability attitudes and bearability attitudes) and Appendix 5 (for help with examining devaluation attitudes and unconditional acceptance attitudes). Again, you need to adapt and apply these arguments to the attitudes you are examining.

   You should now be ready to commit to acting and thinking in ways consistent with your general flexible/non-extreme attitude.

Step 7: Adopt a healthy orientation towards reciprocity in close relationships and its absence

Once you have committed yourself to strengthening your conviction in your general flexible/non-extreme attitude, it is useful for you to develop what I call a healthy orientation towards reciprocity in relationships and, in particular, its absence. This involves you doing the following:

- Recognise that there is nothing intrinsically wrong with wanting reciprocity in relationships. However, it is also important to acknowledge that what you want from a relationship with a person may not be the same as what they want from a relationship with you.

◉ Recognise that most of the time when you act fairly towards others, they will act fairly towards you. In other words, fair treatment tends to yield fair treatment. However, this is certainly not a universal rule and sometimes people close to you will take advantage of your good nature and betray your trust and otherwise treat you unfairly. It is important that you don't add disturbance to this adversity by demanding that the reciprocity effect must exist in such situations. It doesn't and no amount of demanding that it must will make it so. Rather, look at the situation from your flexible/non-extreme mind. When you do so you, will still feel very badly about it (i.e., sorrow), but you won't be disturbed (i.e., hurt).

Step 8: Face your hurt-related theme in imagery

I hope that you have made a commitment to act on your general flexible/non-extreme attitudes. Assuming that you have, your basic task is to face up to others treating you badly (where you think you do not deserve such treatment) and relationship devaluation (where someone indicates that their relationship with you is less important to them than the relationship is to you) and to learn to think in a flexible/non-extreme way about it.

Up to this point, you have worked at a general level with respect to your hurt-related theme, dealing with the general rigid/extreme attitudes that account for your hurt and developing your alternative general flexible/non-extreme attitudes. However, when you come to apply your general flexible/non-extreme attitudes in dealing with others treating you badly (where you think you do not deserve such treatment) and with relationship devaluation (where someone indicates that their relationship with you is less important to them than the relationship is to you), you need to bear in mind one important point. Since you make yourself hurt about specific events (actual or imagined), you need to deal with these by rehearsing specific variants of your general flexible/non-extreme attitudes.

While the best way to do this is in specific situations where others treat you badly (where you think you do not deserve such treatment) and where your relationship is devalued (where someone indicates that their relationship with you is less important to them than the relationship is to you),

you may derive benefit by using imagery first. If this is the case, you need to do the following:

- Imagine a specific situation in which you felt hurt or may feel hurt about (a) others treating you badly (where you think you do not deserve such treatment) or (b) where someone indicates that their relationship with you is less important to them than the relationship is to you and focus, in your mind's eye, on what you felt most hurt about (i.e., your 'A'). Focus on this 'A' while rehearsing a specific flexible/non-extreme attitude relevant to the situation. As you do this, try to make yourself feel sorrowful, rather than hurt.

- Then, see yourself acting in ways consistent with your flexible/non-extreme attitude, e.g., expressing your sorrow, asking the other person for their perspective and engaging the other person in a productive dialogue.

- Recognise that some of your post-rigid/extreme-attitude thinking may be distorted. Respond to it without getting bogged down doing so. Accept the presence of any remaining distorted thoughts without engaging with them.

- Repeat the above steps until you feel sufficiently ready to put this sequence into practice in your life.

If you find that facing your hurt-related 'A', in your mind's eye, is too much for you, use the 'challenging, but not overwhelming' principle that I introduced in Chapter 2 (see p. 33). This means that, instead of imagining yourself facing a hurt-related situation that you find 'overwhelming' at the present time, choose a similar hurt-related 'A' that you would find 'challenging, but not overwhelming'. Then employ the same steps that I have outlined above. Work in this way with modified hurt-related 'A's' until you find your original one 'challenging, but not overwhelming' and then use the steps again.

Step 9: Face people who have treated you unfairly, disclose your sorrow and have a constructive conversation about the experience

Once you have got yourself into a flexible/non-extreme frame of mind about situations about which you felt hurt so that you now feel sorrowful about it, you are in a position to tell people how you healthily feel about what they did or did not do. As you do so, it is important that you don't blame them for the feelings of hurt that you initially felt when you held rigid/extreme attitudes towards their behaviour or its lack. Once you do this, be ready to listen to their response and try to understand them from their perspective. If you do so, they may well let go of their defensiveness and they also may, and I stress the word 'may' here, apologise for their behaviour. However, even if they don't apologise, once you hold flexible/non-extreme attitudes towards their unfair behaviour (for example) rather than rigid/extreme attitudes, you have more of a chance of having a constructive dialogue over the episode and of coming to a constructive resolution.

Step 10: Capitalise on what you have learned

When you have faced a situation in which you experienced hurt and dealt with it as best you could, it is important that you reflect on what you did and what you learned. In particular, if you were able to face the situation, and rehearse your specific flexible/non-extreme attitudes until you felt sorrow, ask yourself how you can capitalise on what you achieved. If you experienced any problems, respond to the following questions:

⊙ Did I face the situation and, if not, why not?

⊙ Did I rehearse my flexible/non-extreme attitudes before, during or after facing the situation and, if not, why not?

⊙ Did I execute my plan to face the situation and, if not, why not?

⊙ Did I engage with post-rigid/extreme attitude distorted thinking and, if so, why?

Reflect on your experience and put into practice what you have learned the next time you face a situation in which someone treats you badly (and you think you do not deserve such treatment) and where someone has devalued your relationship by indicating that their relationship with you is less important to them than the relationship is to you.

Step 11: Generalise your learning

Once you have dealt with your hurt in a specific situation by holding the relevant specific version of your general flexible/non-extreme attitude and by acting and thinking in ways that are consistent with it, you can generalise this learning to situations defined by your hurt-based theme.

Gina was particularly prone to hurt about others with whom she was close neglecting her. Thus:

- Gina assessed the three components of her hurt response and set goals with respect to all three components.

- She identified her relevant general rigid/extreme attitude regarding being neglected (i.e., 'I must not be neglected by those close to me and, if I am, I am unlovable') that underpinned her hurt response and her alternative general flexible/non-extreme attitude (i.e., 'I don't want to be neglected by those close to me, but that does not mean that it must not happen. If it does, it is unfortunate, but it does not prove that I am unlovable. I am the same person whether or not they neglect me') that underpinned her sorrow response.

- She examined both elements of her general rigid/extreme attitude and her general flexible/non-extreme attitude until she clearly saw that the former were false, made no sense and were detrimental to her, and that the latter were true, sensible and healthy.

- She acted on shortened versions of her flexible/non-extreme attitudes in specific situations and disclosed her feelings of sorrow about being neglected. This resulted in a useful discussion with the other, which sometimes resulted in them apologising to her and taking her less for granted in the future.

- As she acted on her flexible/non-extreme attitudes, she tolerated the discomfort that she felt and accepted that some of her distorted and skewed negative thinking would still be in her mind as she did so. She let such thinking be without engaging with it, suppressing it or distracting herself from it.

As this section shows, you can generalise what you learn about dealing with hurt from situation to situation as defined by your hurt-based inference.

USING REBT'S ABCD FORM TO DEAL WITH SPECIFIC EXAMPLES OF YOUR HURT

This chapter is mainly geared to help you deal with your hurt in general terms. However, you can also use this material to address specific examples of your hurt. I have developed a self-help form to provide the structure to assist you in this regard. It is called the ABCD form and it appears with instructions in Appendix 6.

OTHER IMPORTANT ISSUES IN DEALING WITH HURT

In the above section, I outlined an 11-step programme to deal with hurt. In this section, I discuss some other important issues that may be relevant to you in your work to become less prone to this emotional problem. If you want to, you can incorporate them as additional steps in the above step-by-step guide at points relevant to you.

Dealing with your safety-seeking measures to avoid hurt

I mentioned in Chapter 2 that people use safety-seeking measures to protect themselves from threat. You may use similar measures to protect yourself from feeling hurt. Here is how this works from your perspective. You reason that, since you feel hurt about (a) others treating you unfairly and (b) relationship devaluation (where someone indicates that their relationship with you is less important to them than the relationship is to you), you will take one major step to avoid hurt. This involves you keeping yourself at a distance from others to whom you would like to get close and not putting yourself in a position where you feel vulnerable to be taken advantage of. Adopting this position means that you will have superficial relationships with people and will thus be unhappy and frustrated since you ideally want to be closer to them.

However, this stance and the reasoning that leads you to take it are flawed and will only serve to perpetuate your tendency to feel hurt. This is due to the fact that your hurt is not based on (a) others treating you badly (when you think you do not deserve such treatment) or (b) relationship devaluation (where someone indicates that their relationship with you is less important to them than the relationship is to you), but on your rigid/ extreme attitudes towards these two inferences. So, if you want to deal effectively with hurt, you need to do the following:

- Take healthy risks and allow yourself to get close to people and to feel vulnerable. However, do this while holding flexible/non-extreme attitudes towards the above inferences.

- If it transpires that some people do treat you badly or show that they do not value the relationship as much as you do, deal with this by bringing to such situations appropriate specific versions of your general flexible/non-extreme attitudes so that you feel sorrow and not hurt about these episodes. Also, act and think in ways that are consistent with these specific flexible/non-extreme attitudes as far as you can.

If you do this, you will be less likely to keep your distance from those to whom you would like to get close.

Why you feel hurt much of the time and how to deal with this

If you are particularly prone to hurt, you hold the following attitude, which I call a 'chronic hurt-based general rigid/extreme attitude':

- 'Once I invest in people close to me, I must get, and see clearly that I am getting, a fair return on that investment and, if I don't, it's terrible and proves that I am unworthy or to be pitied.'

Holding this attitude, you will do the following:

- You will often focus on past relationships where (a) others have treated you unfairly or (b) where their investment in your relationship was not as strong as yours.

- You scan your current relationships certain to find evidence that others are treating you badly or that they don't care for you as much as you care for them. If there is any ambiguity about this, you err on the side of undeserved treatment and relationship devaluation.

- Finally, as we have seen, you will avoid getting close to people because you are sure that, in your terms, they will hurt you.

How to deal with chronic hurt

In order to deal with this chronic sense of hurt, you need to develop and apply an alternative general flexible/non-extreme attitude that protects you from such hurt:

- 'Once I invest in people close to me, I really want to get, and see clearly that I am getting, a fair return on that investment, but I don't have to do so. If I don't, it's bad, but not terrible and it neither proves that I am unworthy nor to be pitied. Rather, I am a non-poor, fallible human being who has been treated poorly.'

Such an attitude will lead you to think that the following occurred only when there is clear evidence for making such an inference:

- Someone did take advantage of your good nature and treated you unfairly.
- The other person does not value your relationship with you as much as you value your relationship with them.

When there is such evidence, you will feel sorrow rather than hurt because you will be processing this with a specific flexible/non-extreme attitude.

In addition, this attitude will help you to think of times in the past when others did treat you fairly and reciprocated your positive feelings about the relationship as well as helping you to see the potential for good (and bad) in future relationships.

How to examine the accuracy of your hurt-related inference, if necessary

If you are still unsure whether people have treated you badly or do not reciprocate the value you put on your relationship with them, answer one or more of the following questions:

- How valid is my inference that the other person has betrayed me (for example)?

- Would an objective jury agree that the other person betrayed has me? If not, what would the jury's verdict be?

- Is my inference that the other person has betrayed me realistic? If not, what is a more realistic inference?

- If I asked someone whom I could trust to give me an objective opinion about my inference that the other person has betrayed me, what would that person say to me and why? What inference would this person encourage me to make instead?

- If a friend had told me that they had made the same inference about being betrayed in the same situation, what would I say to them about the validity of their inference and why? What inference would I encourage the person to make instead?

Assessing and dealing with emotional problems about hurt

In previous chapters, I discussed the concept of meta-disturbance (literally disturbance about disturbance). It is important to assess carefully the nature of this meta-disturbance about hurt before you can best deal with it.

The best way to start dealing with the assessment of any emotional problems you might have about hurt is to ask yourself the question: 'How do I feel about my feeling of hurt?' The most common emotional problems that people have about hurt are as follows: anxiety, depression, unhealthy regret, shame and unhealthy self-anger. I refer you to the relevant chapters on these emotional problems in this book for help on how to deal with meta-emotional problems about hurt.

Developing and rehearsing non-hurt, sorrow-based world views

People develop views of the world as it relates to them that make it more or less likely that they will experience UNEs. The world views that render you vulnerable to hurt do so in a similar way to the chronic hurt-based general rigid/extreme attitude discussed above (i.e., 'Once I invest in people close to me, I must get a fair return on that investment and, if I don't, it's terrible and proves that I am unworthy or to be pitied') by making you focus unduly on times when you have been, are or will be treated unfairly by others or when your feelings were not, are not or will not be reciprocated in your relationships with others. However, these hurt-based world views have this effect on you much more widely.

It is important that you develop realistic views of the world that will help you to deal with hurt and experience healthy sorrow instead. In Table 7.1, you will find an illustrative list of such world views rather than an exhaustive one, so you can get an idea of what I mean, which will enable you to develop your own. In Table 7.1, I first describe a world view that renders you vulnerable to hurt and then I give its healthy alternative. You will see that the former views are characterised by a conception of significant others as being basically malevolent (e.g., withholding, unfair, excluding, neglectful) individuals who will betray your trust. In the latter

Table 7.1 World views that render you vulnerable to hurt and help you to deal with hurt

Views of the world that render you vulnerable to hurt	Views of the world that help you deal with hurt
⊙ When I do a lot for those close to me, they will fail to reciprocate and will abuse my generosity	⊙ When I do a lot for people, most will reciprocate, but some won't and some may even abuse my generosity
⊙ If I trust those close to me, they will often betray me while I would not betray them	⊙ If I trust those close to me, most won't betray me, but some may well do so
⊙ Significant others will act unfairly towards me while I would not be unfair to them	⊙ Some significant others will indeed act unfairly to me, but not all will. Can I really be sure that I would not act unfairly to them?
⊙ Those close to me will often exclude or neglect me for no good reason	⊙ Those close to me may sometimes exclude or neglect me, but most won't. When they do, I may not understand why, but this does not mean that they have done so for no good reason

views, a more benign, balanced, but realistic picture of others is revealed and thus a healthier response to their unfair treatment can be expected.

If you hold flexible/non-extreme attitudes that are consistent with the views of the world listed on the right-hand side of Table 7.1, and if you act and think in ways that are, in turn, consistent with these flexible/non-extreme attitudes, you will become less prone to hurt.

In Chapter 8, I discuss unhealthy anger and how to deal with it.

Dealing with unhealthy anger

In this chapter, I begin by presenting REBT's way of understanding unhealthy anger and then address how to deal with this very common emotional problem.

UNDERSTANDING UNHEALTHY ANGER

In understanding unhealthy anger, we need to know what we tend to make ourselves unhealthily angry about (i.e., its major inference themes), what attitudes we hold, how we act or tend to act, and how we think when we are unhealthily angry.

Major inference themes in unhealthy anger

When you are unhealthily angry, your anger is about one or more of the following:

- You have been frustrated in some way.
- Your movement towards an important goal has been obstructed in some way.
- Someone has transgressed one of your personal rules.
- You have transgressed one of your own personal rules.
- Someone has shown you disrespect.
- Someone or something has threatened your self-esteem.

Rigid/extreme attitudes

As I explained in Chapter 1, according to REBT, an inference on its own does not account for your emotional problem of unhealthy anger. It is possible

DOI: 10.4324/9781003424307-8

for you to make the same inference and be healthily rather than unhealthily angry. In order for you to feel unhealthily angry when you make one of the six inferences listed above, you have to hold a rigid/extreme attitude. While the rigid attitude is at the core of unhealthy anger, the extreme attitudes that are derived from the rigid attitude often distinguish between whether you are experiencing ego unhealthy anger (where you devalue yourself) or non-ego unhealthy anger (where you 'awfulise', find the adversity unbearable or devalue another person). You may, of course, experience both ego unhealthy anger and non-ego unhealthy anger in a given situation.

Behaviour associated with unhealthy anger

When you hold a rigid/extreme attitude towards one of the six things that people make themselves angry about (see p. 144), you feel unhealthy anger and you will act or tend to act in a number of ways, the most common of which are as follows:

- You attack the other(s) physically.
- You attack the other(s) verbally.
- You attack the other(s) passive-aggressively.
- You displace the attack onto another person, animal or object.
- You withdraw aggressively.
- You recruit allies against the other(s).

You will see from the above list that the main purpose of most of these behaviours (and action tendencies) is to destroy or avoid the person who you think (albeit wrongly) has made you angry. However, such destructive or avoidance behaviour is largely responsible for the maintenance of unhealthy anger, since it prevents you from facing up to the situation in which you make yourself unhealthily angry and from dealing with the issues involved in a healthy manner.

Thinking associated with unhealthy anger

When you hold a rigid/extreme attitude towards an anger-related inference, you will feel unhealthily angry and think in a number of ways.

Remember what I said in Chapter 1: the thinking that accompanies your unhealthy anger is the result of your inference being processed by your rigid/extreme attitude and therefore it is likely to contain a number of thinking errors that I present in Appendix 1. I list the main features of this post-rigid/extreme attitude unhealthy anger-based thinking below:

⊙ You overestimate the extent to which the other(s) acted deliberately.

⊙ You see malicious intent in the motives of the other(s).

⊙ You see yourself as definitely right and the other(s) as definitely wrong.

⊙ You are unable to see the point of view of the other(s).

⊙ You plot to exact revenge.

⊙ You ruminate about the other's behaviour and imagine coming out on top.

It is important to note that such post-rigid/extreme-attitude thinking in unhealthy anger may be in words or in mental images.

HOW TO DEAL WITH UNHEALTHY ANGER

If you are prone to unhealthy anger, you tend to experience this emotional problem in a variety of different settings and in response to a variety of anger-related inferences. Here is how to deal with unhealthy anger so that you become less prone to it.

Step 1: Identify reasons why unhealthy anger is a problem for you and why you want to change

While most UNEs are generally regarded as problematic, this is less so when it comes to unhealthy anger. Indeed, often people whose anger meets the criteria for unhealthy anger (i.e., it leads to largely unconstructive results and leaves them preoccupied with whatever it is that they are unhealthily angry about) are ambivalent about seeing their anger as a problem and thus targeting it for change. If this is true for you, this may be due to two major factors:

⊙ You may not understand what constitutes healthy anger.

⊛ Even when you understand the differences between healthy and unhealthy anger, you may construe unhealthy anger positively and/or healthy anger negatively.

Let me now discuss these two points more fully.

Understanding the differences between unhealthy anger and healthy anger

In this book, I have consistently made the point that the differences between UNEs and HNEs reside not in the inferences that you make about situations in which you find yourself, but in the attitudes that you hold towards these inferences and in the way you subsequently think and act. With respect to anger, then, it is particularly important that you have a clear idea what constitutes healthy anger and, in particular, what are the behaviours and modes of thinking that accompany this healthy form of anger. I refer you to p. 152 for a review. Then compare these responses to those that accompany unhealthy anger (see p. 145 and p. 146). You should ideally see that, in the main, healthy anger is more constructive for you in the longer term than unhealthy anger. If not, you may need to identify and investigate your positive connotations of unhealthy anger and negative connotations of healthy anger.

Identifying and responding to your positive connotations of unhealthy anger and your negative connotations of healthy anger

Having understood the differences between unhealthy anger and healthy anger, you may find yourself drawing back from making a commitment to working towards becoming healthily rather than unhealthily angry. The reasons for this may be due to how you construe both types of anger. These constructions are likely to be based on misconceptions of these different anger types.

Common positive connotations of unhealthy anger

Here are two examples of commonly found positive connotations of unhealthy anger that people tend to make, which stop them from committing to healthy anger as a constructive alternative to their unhealthy anger. I list each positive connotation and then briefly discuss how to respond to it.

- *'When I feel unhealthy anger, I feel powerful and I don't want to lose that feeling.'*

   Response: the power that you experience is based on the attitude of a tyrant (e.g., 'Things have to be my way'). You can experience a different form of power related to being assertive and flexible with healthy anger.

- *'My unhealthy anger is an appropriately strong response to someone breaking one of my most important rules.'*

   Response: Healthy anger can be strong without the destructive effects of unhealthy anger.

Common negative connotations of healthy anger

Here are two examples of commonly found negative connotations of healthy anger that again stop people from committing to healthy anger. As before, I list each negative connotation and then briefly discuss how to respond to it.

- *'Healthy anger is weak and wishy-washy.'*

   Response: While never as strong as blind rage, healthy anger can be very strong and can be based on firmness.

- *'If you are healthily angry, you let people get away with acting badly.'*

   Response: No, you don't. You tell them in no uncertain terms how you feel about their bad behaviour and you apply the necessary consequences, but without damning them.

Step 2: Take responsibility for your unhealthy anger

In REBT, we argue that people or things do not make you unhealthily angry; rather you create these feelings by the rigid/extreme attitudes that you hold towards such people and things. You may object that this involves you blaming yourself for creating your feelings of unhealthy anger, but this objection is based on a misconception. It assumes that taking responsibility for creating your unhealthy anger is synonymous with self-blame. In truth, responsibility means that you take ownership for the rigid/extreme attitudes that underpin your unhealthy anger while accepting yourself for doing so. Blame, on the other Hand, means that you regard yourself as being bad for creating your own unhealthy anger.

Step 3: Identify the themes about which you tend to feel unhealthy anger

You should now be in a position to commit yourself to working towards experiencing healthy anger rather than unhealthy anger. As the object of your unhealthy anger may be yourself, others or aspects of life that do not relate to yourself or others, your anger-related inferences exist in each of these realms of your personal domain. I will group them as such.

Anger-related inferences concerning self

When you are unhealthily angry with yourself, you consider that you either have broken or failed to live up to one of your own personal rules concerning your behaviour. What differentiates unhealthy self-anger from depression is that, in unhealthy anger, you want to attack yourself angrily more than you do in depression. What differentiates unhealthy self-anger from shame and guilt is that, in the latter, your rules concern your moral and socially acceptable behaviour, while, in the former, they tend to be less concerned with the social or moral world and more concerned with the non-moral rules that you have created for yourself.

Anger-related inferences concerning others

As with anxiety, it is useful to ask yourself when you are unhealthily angry with others whether they are, in your mind, threatening your self-esteem or not. Let me first outline the inferences that you make that are relevant to self-esteem when you are unhealthily angry. These threats are experienced more in the here and now than is the case with anxiety.

Common threats to self-esteem in unhealthy anger towards others

Here you infer that the other person has:

⊙ disrespected you;

- criticised you;
- made you look stupid; and
- rejected you.

Common anger-related inferences about others that do not involve threats to your self-esteem

Here you infer that the other person has:

- broken your personal rule concerning how people are to behave;
- failed to live up to your personal rule about how others are to behave;
- blocked your path towards an important goal; and
- frustrated you.

Common anger-related inferences about inanimate objects

- The object frustrates you (e.g., it does not work properly).
- The object blocks your path towards an important goal (e.g., a ticket machine does not issue you with a ticket so that you can't travel and get to an important meeting).

Step 4: Identify the three components of your unhealthy anger response and set goals with respect to each component

The next step is for you to list the three elements of your unhealthy anger response in the face of each of the themes listed above.

Identify the three components of your unhealthy anger response

I use the term 'unhealthy anger response' to describe the three main components that make up this response. The three components of your unhealthy anger response are the emotional, behavioural and thinking components.

Emotional component

The emotional component is, of course, unhealthy anger.

Behavioural component

The behavioural component concerns overt behaviour or action tendencies. These will be largely attacking in nature. Consult the list that I provided to help you identify your behaviour associated with each theme when you are unhealthily angry (see p. 145). It is important to note that we are often taught to suppress our tendency to act in ways that are consistent with our unhealthy anger. This is why identifying such suppressed behavioural tendencies is often a more reliable guide to the fact that your anger is unhealthy than your actual behaviour will be.

Thinking component

The thinking component of your unhealthy anger often concerns fantasies of getting even and gaining revenge. Such behaviour reflects how you would like to respond if you did not suppress your actual behaviour and your action tendencies. Whereas, in unhealthy behaviour, you can frequently be said to be prosocial in your actual behaviour in that you will not give full behavioural expression to what you would like to do, in your thinking you are antisocial in that your thoughts and images often express the full extent of your wish to get back at the person or object that, in your mind, has angered you.

Set goals with respect to each of the three components

You need to set goals so that you know what you are striving for when you deal effectively with unhealthy anger. The three goals are emotional, behavioural and thinking goals.

Emotional goal

Your emotional goal is healthy anger rather than unhealthy anger (or whatever synonym you prefer to the term 'healthy anger'). Healthy anger is an HNE, which is an appropriate response to the anger-related inferences I outlined earlier, but one that helps you to process what has happened to you and move on with your life rather than get stuck or bogged down.

Behavioural goal

Your behavioural goal should reflect actions that are based on healthy anger rather than unhealthy anger. The following are the most common behaviours associated with healthy anger. You may wish to compare these behaviours with those associated with unhealthy anger that I presented on p. 145.

⊙ You assert yourself with the other(s).

⊙ You request, but do not demand, behavioural change from the other(s).

⊙ You leave an unsatisfactory situation non-aggressively after taking steps to deal with it.

Thinking goal

As well as setting behavioural goals related to the feeling of healthy anger in the face of anger-related inferences, it is important that you set thinking goals associated with this emotion. The following are the most common forms of thinking associated with healthy anger rather than unhealthy anger. Again, you may wish to compare these forms of thinking with those associated with unhealthy anger that I presented on p. 146.

⊙ You think that the other(s) may have acted deliberately, but you also recognise that this may not have been the case.

⊙ You are able to see the point of view of the other(s).

⊙ You have fleeting rather than sustained thoughts to exact revenge.

⊙ You think that other(s) may have had malicious intent in their motives, but you also recognise that this may not have been the case.

⊙ You think that you are probably rather than definitely right and the other(s) are probably rather than definitely wrong.

As the above list shows, the dominant feature of thinking associated with healthy anger is that it is realistic and balanced. Please remember that such thinking may be in words or in mental pictures.

Step 5: Identify your general rigid/extreme attitudes and alternative general flexible/non-extreme attitudes

A general rigid/extreme attitude is a rigid/extreme attitude that you hold across situations defined by the anger-related inference theme(s) to which you are vulnerable. It accounts for your unhealthy anger response. Its flexible/non-extreme alternative, which will also be general in nature, will account for your healthy anger response.

Identify your general rigid/extreme attitudes

When you identify a general rigid/extreme attitude, you take a common anger-related theme (e.g., threat to your self-esteem or someone breaking your personal rule) and add to this a general rigid attitude and the main extreme attitude that is derived from the rigid attitude.

When you are particularly prone to self-esteem based unhealthy anger, your main extreme attitude will be an other-devaluation attitude when your focus is on the other person who threatened your self-esteem, but you will also have an underlying self-devaluation attitude.

For non-self-esteem based unhealthy anger, your main extreme attitude will frequently be an other-devaluation attitude (when the focus of your unhealthy anger is others) or it may be an unbearability or a life-devaluation attitude (particular when the focus of your unhealthy anger is inanimate objects or frustrating life conditions). For example:

- 'People must not put me down. If they do, I am inadequate' (a general self-esteem based rigid/extreme attitude).

- 'People must keep their promises and they are bad if they don't' (a general non-self-esteem based rigid/extreme attitude).

Identify your alternative general flexible/non-extreme attitudes

When you identify your alternative general flexible/non-extreme attitude, you take the same common theme (e.g., the threat to your self-esteem or someone breaking your personal rule) and add to this a general flexible attitude and the main non-extreme attitude that is derived from the flexible attitude.

If your general extreme attitude was self-devaluation (when you are particularly prone to self-esteem based unhealthy anger), your general non-extreme attitude will be an unconditional self-acceptance attitude. If you are prone to non-self-esteem based unhealthy anger, your alternative general non-extreme attitudes will be an other-acceptance attitude, a bearability attitude or an unconditional acceptance attitude towards another or life. For example:

- 'I don't want people to put me down, but that does not mean that they must not do so. If they do, I am not inadequate and they are not bad. We are both fallible human beings who can act in a myriad of different ways, both good and bad' (a general unconditional self-acceptance based on a flexible/non-extreme attitude).

- 'I want people to keep their promises, but unfortunately they don't have to do so. If they don't, it's bad, but they are not. They are fallible and capable of acting well and badly' (a general unconditional other-acceptance based on a flexible/non-extreme attitude).

Step 6: Examine your general attitudes

While there are many ways of examining your general rigid/extreme attitudes and general flexible/non-extreme attitudes, in my view the most efficient way involves you first examining together your general rigid attitude and its general flexible attitude alternative, and then examining together your general extreme attitude and its general non-extreme attitude alternative.

Examine your general rigid attitude and its general flexible attitude alternative

First, take your general rigid attitude and its general flexible attitude alternative and write them down next to one another on a sheet of paper. Then ask yourself:

- Which is true and which is false?

- Which is sensible logically and which does not make sense?

- Which has largely constructive results and which has largely unconstructive results?

Write down your answer to each of these questions on your piece of paper, giving reasons for each answer. Consult Appendix 2 for help with the answers to these questions, which you need to adapt and apply to the attitudes you are examining.

Examine your general extreme attitude and its general non-extreme attitude alternative

Next, take your general extreme attitude and its general non-extreme attitude alternative and again write them down next to one another on a sheet of paper. Then, ask yourself the same three questions that you used with your general rigid attitude and its general flexible attitude alternative. Again, write down your answer to each of these questions on your piece of paper, giving reasons for each answer. I suggest that you consult Appendix 3 (for help with examining awfulising and non-awfulising attitudes), Appendix 4 (for help with examining unbearability attitudes and bearability attitudes) and Appendix 5 (for help with examining devaluation attitudes and unconditional acceptance attitudes). Again, you need to adapt and apply these arguments to the attitudes you are examining.

You should now be ready to commit to act and think in ways consistent with your general flexible/non-extreme attitude.

Step 7: Face your unhealthy anger-related theme in imagery

I hope that you have made a commitment to act and think in ways that are consistent with your general flexible/non-extreme attitudes. Assuming that you have, your basic task is to face up to your anger-related theme while rehearsing your flexible/non-extreme attitudes.

Up to this point, you have worked at a general level with respect to the anger-related themes about which you are unhealthily angry, the general rigid/extreme attitudes that account for this unhealthy anger and their alternative general flexible/non-extreme attitudes. However, when you come to apply your general flexible/non-extreme attitudes in dealing with your response to these themes, you need to bear in mind one important point. Since you make yourself unhealthily angry in specific situations (actual or imagined), you need to deal with these specific situations by rehearsing specific variants of your general flexible/non-extreme attitudes.

While the best way to do this is in specific situations in which you infer threat to your self-esteem or where others have broken your personal rules, you may derive benefit from using imagery first. If this is the case with you, you need to do the following:

◉ Imagine a specific situation in which you felt unhealthily angry and focus on what you were most angry about.

◉ See yourself facing what you were most angry about while rehearsing a specific flexible/non-extreme attitude relevant to the situation. As you do this, try to make yourself feel healthily angry, rather than unhealthily angry.

◉ Then see yourself take assertive action. Make your picture realistic. Picture a faltering performance rather than a masterful one.

◉ Recognise that some of your post-rigid/extreme-attitude thinking may be distorted. Respond to it without getting bogged down doing so. Accept the presence of any remaining distorted thoughts without engaging with them.

◉ Repeat the above steps until you feel sufficiently ready to put this sequence into practice in your life.

If you find that facing your anger-related inference theme, in your mind's eye, is too much for you, use a principle that I call 'challenging, but not overwhelming' that I introduced in Chapter 2 (see p. 33). This means that, instead of imagining yourself facing a situation about which you would make yourself overwhelmingly angry, choose a similar situation in which you would make yourself unhealthily angry, but not overwhelmingly so. Then employ the same steps that I have outlined above. Work in this way until you feel able to face what you were previously overwhelmingly angry about and then use the steps again.

Step 8: Act assertively in relevant anger-related situations

Whether or not you have used imagery as a preparatory step, you need to take the following steps when you assert yourself in anger-related situations.

◉ Choose a specific situation that contains the theme about which you are likely to make yourself unhealthily angry.

◉ Make a plan of how you are going to assert yourself in the situation.

- Rehearse a specific version of your general flexible/non-extreme attitudes before entering the situation so that you can face what you are angry about while in a flexible/non-extreme frame of mind. In addition, it would be useful to develop a shorthand version of your specific flexible/non-extreme attitude to use while you are in the situation.

- Enter the situation and accept the fact that you are likely to be uncomfortable while doing so. Assert yourself as previously planned. React to any consequences from a flexible/non-extreme frame of mind if you can.

- Recognise that, even though you have got yourself into a flexible/non-extreme frame of mind, some of your thinking may be distorted and unrealistic and some may be realistic and balanced. Accept the presence of the former and do not engage with it. Engage with the latter as much as you can.

Step 9: Capitalise on what you learned

When you have faced the situation and dealt with it as best you could, it is important that you reflect on what you did and what you learned. In particular, if you were able to face the relevant theme, rehearse your specific flexible/non-extreme attitudes and assert yourself, ask yourself how you can capitalise on what you achieved. If you experienced any problems, respond to the following questions:

- Did I focus on the aspect of the situation that I was unhealthily angry about and, if not, why not?

- Did I rehearse my flexible/non-extreme attitudes before and during facing what I was unhealthily angry about and, if not, why not?

- Did I assert myself and, if not, why not?

- Did I engage with post-rigid/extreme attitude distorted thinking and, if so, why?

Reflect on your experience and put into practice what you have learned the next time you face what you are unhealthily angry about.

Step 10: Generalise your learning

While you can really deal with your unhealthy anger only in specific situations, you can generalise what you have learned about dealing effectively with unhealthy anger across situations defined by an anger-related theme to which you are particularly vulnerable (e.g., people breaking your personal rules) and also apply your learning to situations defined by a different theme that you may have problems with (e.g., frustration).

Clare was particularly prone to unhealthy anger about other people cancelling arrangements at the last minute, so she followed the steps outlined in this chapter. Thus:

- Clare assessed the three components of her unhealthy anger response and set goals with respect to all three components.

- She identified her relevant general rigid/extreme attitude regarding her rule for people keeping arrangements with her (i.e., 'People must not cancel arrangements with me at the last minute and, if they do, they are bad people') that underpinned her unhealthy anger response and her alternative general flexible/non-extreme attitude (i.e., 'I don't want people to cancel arrangements with me at the last minute, but they don't have to do what I want them to do. It's bad that they have done the wrong thing, but they are not bad for doing so. They are fallible human beings who are acting badly') that underpinned her healthy anger response.

- She examined both elements of her general rigid/extreme attitude and her general flexible/non-extreme attitude until she clearly saw that the former were false, made no sense and were detrimental to her, and that the latter were true, sensible and healthy.

- She outlined situations where she thought other people were likely to cancel on her and used imagery to practise specific versions of her flexible/non-extreme attitudes while focusing on the other person cancelling on her. She did this until she felt healthily angry. She then used these skills in actual relevant situations. She used shortened versions of her flexible/non-extreme attitude (i.e., 'It's bad, but they are fallible') as she asserted herself with the other person and told them that she did not like their behaviour and hoped that they would not cancel late again. As she used her assertive skills, she tolerated the discomfort that she felt and accepted that some of her 'post-rigid/extreme attitude' thinking would still be in her mind as she did so. She let such thinking be without engaging with it, suppressing it or distracting herself from it.

- When she had made progress in dealing with her unhealthy anger about such cancellations, she applied these skills to dealing with her discomfort-related unhealthy anger with respect to people frustrating her in shops and other public settings.

- She identified her relevant general rigid/extreme attitude regarding frustration (i.e., 'They must not frustrate me and I can't bear it when they do') that underpinned her unhealthy anger response and her alternative general flexible/non-extreme attitude (i.e., 'I don't want others to frustrate me, but they don't have to do what I want. It's difficult for me to bear such frustration, but I can do so, it's worth it to me to do so and I am worth doing it for') that underpinned her healthy anger response.

- She again examined both elements of her general rigid/extreme attitude and her general flexible/non-extreme attitude until she clearly saw that the former were false, made no sense and were detrimental to her, and that the latter were true, sensible and healthy.

- She then outlined situations that she found particularly frustrating and prepared to face them by examining specific versions of these attitudes. She first rehearsed relevant specific versions of her general flexible/non-extreme attitudes regarding frustration and faced this in these specific situations while keeping in mind a shortened version of her flexible/non-extreme attitude (i.e., 'I can bear being frustrated').

- As she did so, she stayed in the situation and allowed herself to experience her feeling of healthy anger. She accepted that some of her 'unhealthy anger' thinking would still be in her mind as she did so. She again let such thinking be without engaging with it, suppressing it or distracting herself from it.

As this section shows, you can generalise what you learn about dealing with unhealthy anger from situation to situation as defined by a specific anger-related theme and from there to situations defined by a different anger-related theme. If you do this consistently, you will eventually take the toxicity out of the emotional problem of unhealthy anger!

USING REBT'S ABCD FORM TO DEAL WITH SPECIFIC EXAMPLES OF YOUR UNHEALTHY ANGER

This chapter is mainly geared to help you deal with your unhealthy anger in general terms. However, you can also use this material to address specific examples of your unhealthy anger. I have developed a self-help form to provide the structure to assist you in this regard. It is called the ABCD form and it appears with instructions in Appendix 6.

OTHER IMPORTANT ISSUES IN DEALING WITH UNHEALTHY ANGER

In the above section, I outlined a 10-step programme to deal with unhealthy anger. In this section, I discuss some other important issues that may be relevant to you in your work to become less prone to this emotional problem. If you want to, you can incorporate them as additional steps in the above step-by-step guide at points relevant to you.

Why you overestimate the presence of anger-related themes and how to deal with it

If you are particularly prone to unhealthy anger, you will be particularly sensitive to seeing the presence of anger-related themes (such as others showing you disrespect) where others, who are not prone to unhealthy anger, do not. So far in this chapter, I have helped you to deal with unhealthy anger in situations where you infer the presence of anger-related themes. In this section, I help you to understand and deal with situations where you overestimate their presence in the first place. I will use the example where you are particularly prone to infer disrespect in the behaviour of others.

Why you overestimate the presence of disrespect

This is how you come to overestimate the presence of disrespect in the behaviour of others.

⊚ You take the theme of your general rigid/extreme attitude:

Disrespect from the general rigid/extreme attitude: *'I must not be shown disrespect. Others are bad if they do not respect me.'*

⊚ You construct a second general rigid/extreme attitude that features ambiguity about the theme:

'It must be clear that *others respect me. I can't tolerate such ambiguity.'*

- You bring this second general rigid/extreme attitude to situations where it is possible that you may be or have been disrespected and you make an inference about the presence of disrespect because you cannot convince yourself that you have been respected:

'Since it is not clear that you have shown me respect, you have disrespected me.'

- You focus on this inference and bring a specific version of your original general rigid/extreme attitude to this inference. For example:

Inference: *'My boss disrespected me.'*

Specific rigid/extreme attitude: *'My boss must not show me disrespect. He is bad for doing so.'*

How to deal with your overestimations of the presence of disrespect

In order to deal with your overestimations of the presence of disrespect, you need to take a number of steps, which I will illustrate.

- Construct general flexible/non-extreme alternatives to your original disrespect-focused general rigid/extreme attitude:

'I don't want to be disrespected, but that does not mean I must not be disrespected. If I am, it's bad but the person is not bad for doing so. They are fallible.'

And to your second ambiguity-focused general rigid/extreme attitude:

'I would like to have clear evidence that I am respected, but I don't need such clarity. It is difficult not having this clarity, but I can bear not having it and it is worth bearing.'

- Examine both sets of attitudes until you can see the truth, logic and helpful nature of the two general flexible/non-extreme attitudes and the falseness, illogic and unhelpful nature of the two general rigid/extreme attitudes and you can commit to implement the former.

- Bring your ambiguity-focused general flexible/non-extreme attitude to situations where it is possible that you may be or have been disrespected and make an inference based on the data at hand:

'It's not clear if I have been disrespected or not, so let's consider the evidence.'

⊙ If there is evidence indicating there is a good chance that you will be or have been disrespected, use a specific version of your general disrespect-focused flexible/non-extreme attitude to deal with this. For example:

Inference: *'My boss has disrespected me.'*

Specific flexible/non-extreme attitude: *'I don't want my boss to disrespect me, but sadly he does not have to do what I want him to do. It is bad that he did so, but he is not bad. He is a fallible human being who is capable of showing respect and disrespect.'*

How to examine the accuracy of your inference of threat, if necessary

If you are still unsure if your inference of disrespect is accurate or inaccurate, answer one or more of the following questions:

⊙ How likely is it that I was disrespected (or might be disrespected)?

⊙ Would an objective jury agree that I was (or might be) disrespected? If not, what would the jury's verdict be?

⊙ Did I view (am I viewing) the situation in which I inferred disrespect realistically? If not, how could I have viewed (can I view) it more realistically?

⊙ If I asked someone whom I could trust to give me an objective opinion about the truth or falsity of my inference about being disrespected, what would the person say to me and why? What inference would this person encourage me to make instead?

⊙ If a friend had told me that they had faced (were facing or were about to face) the same situation as I faced and had made the same inference of disrespect, what would I say to them about the validity of their inference and why? What inference would I encourage the person to make instead?

Assessing and dealing with emotional problems about unhealthy anger

As I have already pointed out, we have the unique ability to disturb ourselves about our emotional problems. It is important to assess carefully the nature of this meta-disturbance about unhealthy anger before you can best deal with it.

The best way to start dealing with the assessment of any emotional problems you might have about unhealthy anger is to ask yourself the question: 'How do I feel about my feeling of unhealthy anger?' The most common emotional problems that people have about unhealthy anger are as follows: anxiety, depression, guilt, unhealthy regret, shame and unhealthy self-anger. I discuss only unhealthy self-anger about unhealthy anger in this chapter and refer you to the relevant chapters on these emotional problems in this book for help on how to deal with meta-emotional problems about unhealthy anger.

Assessing unhealthy self-anger about unhealthy anger

When you are unhealthily angry with yourself about your unhealthy anger, it is clear that you think that you have broken your own rule about experiencing unhealthy anger. This may be about the whole response itself or one or more of its components (i.e., the feeling component, the behavioural component or the thinking component). In my experience, you are most likely to be unhealthily angry with yourself for what you did (or felt like doing) when you were originally unhealthily angry.

Dealing with unhealthy self-anger about unhealthy anger

Unless you deal with your unhealthy self-anger about unhealthy anger, you are unlikely to deal with your original unhealthy anger. This is because your focus will be on blaming yourself for your anger problem, which will take you away from dealing with this problem.

The best way of dealing with your unhealthy self-anger about your original unhealthy anger is to accept yourself unconditionally for having a problem with unhealthy anger. Yes, you may be breaking one of your personal rules by being unhealthily angry and expressing it in unconstructive ways, but sadly there is no reason why you must not break your rule about being angry or expressing your unhealthy anger. You are human and humans do break their rules. That does not mean that you should not take responsibility for making yourself unhealthily angry in the first place and expressing it unconstructively in the second place. Far from it! Indeed, unless you take responsibility for your unhealthy anger, you won't deal with it. But you can take responsibility without the self-blame that is a central feature of your unhealthy self-anger about your original anger problem.

Developing and rehearsing healthy anger-based world views

People develop views of the world as it relates to them that make it more or less likely that they will experience UNEs. The world views that render you vulnerable to unhealthy anger do so in a similar way to your ambiguity-focused general rigid/extreme attitudes towards a specific anger-related theme – by making you oversensitive to the presence of the theme about which you hold unhealthy anger-related rigid/extreme attitudes. However, these unhealthy anger-based world views have this effect on you much more widely.

It is important that you develop realistic views of the world that will help you to deal with unhealthy anger and experience healthy anger instead. In Table 8.1, you will find an illustrative list of such world views rather

Table 8.1 World views that render you vulnerable to unhealthy anger and help you to deal with unhealthy anger

Views of the world that render you vulnerable to unhealthy anger	Views of the world that help you deal with unhealthy anger
⦿ It's a dog-eat-dog world	⦿ The world is very complex and varied. It can be dog-eat-dog, but it can also be dog-look-after-dog!
⦿ People only selfishly look after themselves and their own	⦿ People look after themselves and their own, but in a self-caring way as well as selfishly. They also look after others as well
⦿ There's no such thing as an accident. People always act with malicious intent	⦿ People can act with malicious intent, but certainly not all the time and accidents do happen
⦿ People are out to get me, so I need to get them before they get me	⦿ People may be out to get me, but they also may be out to help me and be friendly. I don't need to go on the attack unless there is clear evidence that they are out to harm me

than an exhaustive one, so you can get an idea of what I mean, which will enable you to develop your own. In Table 8.1, I first describe a world view that renders you vulnerable to unhealthy anger and then I give its healthy alternative. You will see that the latter views are characterised by complexity and being non-extreme in nature, whereas, in the former, aspects of the world that relate to the anger-related theme are portrayed as unidimensional and extreme.

If you hold flexible/non-extreme attitudes that are consistent with the views of the world listed on the right-hand side of Table 8.1, and if you act and think in ways that are, in turn, consistent with these flexible/non-extreme attitudes, you will become less prone to unhealthy anger.

In Chapter 9, I discuss unhealthy jealousy and how to deal with it.

Dealing with unhealthy jealousy

In this chapter, I begin by presenting REBT's way of understanding unhealthy jealousy and then address how to deal with this emotional problem.

UNDERSTANDING UNHEALTHY JEALOUSY

In understanding unhealthy jealousy, we need to know what we tend to make ourselves unhealthily jealous about (i.e., its major inference themes), what attitudes we hold, how we act or tend to act, and how we think when we are unhealthily jealous.

Major inference themes in unhealthy jealousy

There are two major themes in relation to your personal domain that are implicated in unhealthy jealousy:

- A threat is posed to your relationship with your partner from a third person. While you may experience unhealthy jealousy in relationships that are not romantic in nature, in this chapter I focus on unhealthy jealousy within the context of romantic relationships since it is the most common form of jealousy and it brings out quite vividly how your mind works in this emotional problem.

- A threat is posed by the uncertainty you face concerning your partner's whereabouts, behaviour, thoughts and feelings in the context of the first threat.

Rigid/extreme attitudes

As I explained in Chapter 1, according to REBT, inferences on their own do not account for emotional problems. It is possible, therefore, for you to make the same inferences as listed above and feel healthy jealousy and

DOI: 10.4324/9781003424307-9

not unhealthy jealousy.[1] In order for you to feel unhealthy jealousy, you have to hold a rigid attitude and one or more extreme attitudes. While the rigid attitude is at the core of unhealthy jealousy, the extreme attitudes that are derived from the rigid attitude often distinguish between where you devalue yourself (usually when you compare yourself to your 'rival' or if you were to lose your partner) and where you find the uncertainty of not knowing key aspects to do with your partner unbearable. In chronic unhealthy jealousy, you often hold both a threat-related self-devaluation attitude and an uncertainty-related unbearability attitude in a given situation.

Behaviour associated with unhealthy jealousy

When you hold a rigid/extreme attitude towards a threat that you think is posed by someone else to your relationship and by the uncertainty involved in this threat, you will act or tend to act in a number of ways, the most common of which are as follows:

- You seek constant reassurance that you are loved.

- You monitor the actions and feelings of your partner.

- You search for evidence that your partner is involved with someone else.

- You attempt to restrict the movements or activities of your partner.

- You set tests that your partner has to pass.

- You retaliate for your partner's presumed infidelity.

- You sulk.

Thinking associated with unhealthy jealousy

When you hold a rigid/extreme attitude towards a threat that you think is posed by someone else to your relationship, and you face uncertainty concerning your partner's whereabouts, behaviour or thinking, you will tend to think in a number of ways. Remember what I said in Chapter 1: the thinking that accompanies your unhealthy jealousy is the result of your inference being processed by your rigid/extreme attitude and therefore it is likely to contain a number of thinking errors that I present in Appendix 1. I list the main features of this post-rigid/extreme attitude unhealthy jealousy-based thinking below:

- You exaggerate any threat to your relationship that does exist.

- You think the loss of your relationship is imminent.

- You misconstrue your partner's ordinary conversations with relevant others as having romantic or sexual connotations.

- You construct visual images of your partner's infidelity.

- If your partner admits to finding another person attractive, you think that your partner finds that person more attractive than you and that your partner will leave you for this other person.

As you can see, such thinking exaggerates the negative consequences of the perceived threat to your relationship. Such thinking may be in words or in mental images.

HOW TO DEAL WITH UNHEALTHY JEALOUSY

If you are prone to unhealthy jealousy, you tend to experience this emotional problem in a variety of different settings and in response to a variety of situations where you think someone poses a threat to your relationship. Here is how to deal with unhealthy jealousy so that you become less prone to it.

Step 1: Identify reasons why unhealthy jealousy is a problem for you and why you want to change

While unhealthy jealousy is generally regarded as an emotional problem, it is useful for you to spell out reasons why unhealthy jealousy is a problem for you and why you want to change. I suggest that you keep a written list of these reasons and refer to it as needed as a reminder of why you are engaged in a self-help programme. I discuss the healthy alternative to unhealthy jealousy in Step 4.

Step 2: Take responsibility for your unhealthy jealousy

In REBT, we argue that people do not make you unhealthily jealous; rather you create these feelings by the rigid/extreme attitudes that you hold towards what such people do or do not do. You may object that this view condones other people's behaviour, but this objection is based on a misconception. You can take responsibility for creating your unhealthy jealousy and still not condone others' behaviour when it is clear that they have posed a threat to your relationship.

You may object that this view involves you blaming yourself for creating your feelings, but this objection is also based on a misconception. It assumes that taking responsibility for creating your unhealthy jealousy is synonymous with self-blame. In truth, responsibility means that you take ownership for the rigid/extreme attitudes that underpin your unhealthy jealousy while accepting yourself for doing so. Blame, on the other hand, means that you regard yourself as being bad for creating your own unhealthy jealousy.

Step 3: Identify themes about which you tend to feel unhealthy jealousy

The best way of identifying what you tend to feel unhealthy jealousy about is to understand the major themes associated with unhealthy jealousy and how this theme manifests with respect to your personal domain. As I outlined, one major theme in unhealthy jealousy is when you perceive a risk posed by a third person to your relationship. Such threat might be manifest in the following ways:

- You think that your partner will leave you.

- You think that you are not the most important person in your partner's life.

   Here you think that your partner finds another person more attractive than you and that you will be displaced as the most important person in your partner's life (even though you don't think that your partner will go off with the other person).

⦿ You think that you are not your partner's one and only.

Here, it is important to you that your partner is interested only in you and that your partner's interest in another person means that you are no longer his or her one and only.

⦿ You think that someone is showing an interest in your partner.

Here, it is important to you that no one (who has the potential to be a love rival) shows an interest in your partner, so, when someone does, you deem this to be a threat.

The second major inference theme in your unhealthy jealousy concerns the threat posed by the uncertainty you face concerning your partner's whereabouts, behaviour or thinking in the context of the first threat.

Step 4: Identify the three components of your unhealthy jealousy response and set goals with respect to each component

The next step is for you to list the three elements of your unhealthy jealousy response in the face of each of the relevant themes listed above.

Identify the three components of your unhealthy jealousy response

I use the term 'unhealthy jealousy response' to describe the three main components that make up this response. The three components of your unhealthy jealousy response are the emotional, behavioural and thinking components.

Emotional component

The emotional component here is, of course, unhealthy jealousy.

Behavioural component

The behavioural component concerns overt behaviour or action tendencies that you engage in or 'feel like' engaging in when you feel unhealthy jealousy. Consult the list that I provided to help you identify your behaviour associated with each relevant theme when you feel unhealthy jealousy (see p. 167).

Thinking component

The thinking component associated with unhealthy jealousy is listed on p. 168. Again, these may be in words or in mental pictures. Consult this list if necessary.

Set goals with respect to each of the three components

You need to set goals so that you know what you are striving for when you deal effectively with unhealthy jealousy. The three goals are emotional, behavioural and thinking goals.

Emotional goal

Your emotional goal is healthy jealousy rather than unhealthy jealousy (or whatever synonym you prefer to the term 'healthy jealousy'). Healthy jealousy is an HNE, which is an appropriate response to the threat that you think is being posed to your relationship by a third person and to the threat of uncertainty related to your partner in the context of the first threat. It helps you to think objectively about the situation and your response to it and helps you to move on with your life rather than get stuck or bogged down.

Behavioural goal

Your behavioural goal should reflect actions that are based on healthy jealousy rather than unhealthy jealousy. The following are the most common behaviours associated with healthy jealousy. You may wish to compare these behaviours with those associated with unhealthy jealousy that I presented on p. 167.

- You allow your partner to initiate expressing love for you without prompting him or her or seeking reassurance once your partner has done so.

- You allow your partner freedom without monitoring his or her feelings, actions and whereabouts.

- You allow your partner to show natural sexual interest in others without setting tests.

Thinking goal

As well as setting behavioural goals related to the feeling of healthy jealousy about a threat posed by a third person to your relationship, it is important that you set thinking goals associated with this emotion. The following are the most common forms of thinking associated with healthy jealousy rather than unhealthy jealousy. Again, you may wish to compare these forms of thinking with those associated with unhealthy jealousy that I presented on p. 168.

- You tend not to exaggerate any threat to your relationship that does exist.
- You do not misconstrue ordinary conversations between your partner and another man or woman.
- You do not construct visual images of your partner's infidelity.
- You accept that your partner will find others attractive, but you do not see this as a threat.

As the above list shows, the dominant feature of thinking associated with healthy jealousy is that it is realistic and balanced. Please remember that such thinking may be in words or in mental pictures.

Step 5: Recognise that your symptoms of unhealthy jealousy are evidence of disturbance and not necessarily of the existence of threat to your relationship

Once you have identified your unhealthily jealous response and its healthy alternative, it is important that you realise one important point. If you feel jealous a lot, your feelings and the thoughts that accompany them are most likely to be evidence that you have a jealousy problem rather than proof that there truly exists a threat to your relationship.

When you think that there is a threat to your relationship because you have jealous feelings and jealous thoughts, you are succumbing to two thinking errors known as emotional reasoning and cognitive reasoning. In emotional reasoning, you assume that because you feel jealous, your relationship is under threat. In cognitive reasoning, you think that your jealous thoughts are proof that again your relationship is under threat (e.g., 'Because I think that my partner would much prefer to be with the woman he is talking to rather than with me, then he would, in reality, rather have a relationship with her than me').

If your unhealthy jealousy is chronic, when you have jealous feelings and thoughts your task is to remind yourself that these are, in all probability, signs that you are thinking in rigid/extreme ways and that you need to identify and deal with the rigid/extreme attitudes that underpin your unhealthy jealousy response rather than to act on them. You may well find this difficult, because, when you have jealous feelings and thoughts, you will also experience an urge to act on them. Refraining from doing so will go against the grain and will thus be uncomfortable, but, if you do so, you will put yourself in the position of dealing effectively with your unhealthy jealousy. If you don't, you will maintain this emotional problem.

Step 6: Identify your general rigid/extreme attitudes and alternative general flexible/ non-extreme attitudes

A general rigid/extreme attitude leading to your unhealthy jealousy response is a rigid/extreme attitude that you hold across situations defined by one of the following two themes:

- The threat posed by a third person to your relationship:

- You think that your partner will leave you.

- You think that you are not the most important person in your partner's life.

- You think that you are not your partner's one and only.

- You think that someone is showing an interest in your partner.

- The threat posed by the uncertainty you face concerning your partner's whereabouts, behaviour or thinking in the context of the first threat.

Its flexible/non-extreme alternative, which will also be general in nature, will account for your healthy jealousy response.

Identify your general rigid/extreme attitudes

When you identify a general rigid/extreme attitude, you take a common unhealthy jealousy-related theme (see above) and add to this a general rigid attitude and the main extreme attitude that is derived from the rigid attitude. In unhealthy jealousy, your main extreme attitude will be either an unbearability attitude or a self-devaluation attitude.

Here is an example of a rigid/extreme attitude related to each theme in unhealthy jealousy:

- 'Third person threat' unhealthy jealousy:

    'My partner must not find any other person attractive. If they do, then it proves that I am unlovable.'

- 'Uncertainty threat' unhealthy jealousy:

    'I must know what my partner is thinking when we are in the company of attractive people and I can't bear not knowing.'

Identify your alternative general flexible/non-extreme attitudes

When you identify your alternative general flexible/non-extreme attitude, you take the same common theme (e.g., the threat posed by a third person to your relationship and the threat posed by the uncertainty you face concerning your partner's whereabouts, behaviour or thinking in the context of the first threat) and add to this a general flexible attitude and a general discomfort tolerance attitude or a general unconditional self-acceptance attitude. For example:

- 'Third person threat' healthy jealousy:

    'I don't want my partner to find any other person attractive, but that does not mean that they must not do so. If they do then it is unfortunate, but it does not prove that I am unlovable. I can accept myself as a unique, unrateable, fallible human being whose worth is not changed by my partner finding another person attractive.'

- 'Uncertainty threat' healthy jealousy:

    'I would like to know what my partner is thinking when we are in the company of attractive people, but I don't have to know this. It's a struggle not knowing, but I can bear not knowing and it is worth it to me to do so.'

Step 7: Examine your general attitudes

I recommended in previous chapters that you first examine together your general rigid attitude and its general flexible attitude alternative and then examine together your general extreme attitude and its general non-extreme attitude alternative.

Examine your general rigid attitude and its general flexible attitude alternative

First, take your general rigid attitude and its general flexible attitude alternative and write them down next to one another on a sheet of paper. Then ask yourself:

⊙ Which is true and which is false?

⊙ Which is sensible logically and which does not make sense?

⊙ Which has largely constructive results and which has largely unconstructive results?

Write down your answer to each of these questions on your piece of paper, giving reasons for each answer. Consult Appendix 2 for help with the answers to these questions, which you need to adapt and apply to the attitudes you are examining.

Examine your general extreme attitude and its general non-extreme attitude alternative

Next, take your general extreme attitude and its general non-extreme attitude alternative and again write them down next to one another on a sheet of paper. Then, ask yourself the same three questions that you used with your general rigid attitude and its general flexible attitude alternative. Again, write down your answer to each of these questions on your piece of paper, giving reasons for each answer. I suggest that you consult Appendix 3 (for help with examining awfulising attitudes and non-awfulising attitudes), Appendix 4 (for help with examining unbearability attitudes and bearability tolerance attitudes) and Appendix 5 (for help with examining devaluation attitudes and unconditional acceptance attitudes). Again, you need to adapt and apply these arguments to the attitudes you are examining.

You should now be ready to commit to act and think in ways consistent with your general flexible/non-extreme attitude.

Step 8: Face your unhealthy jealousy-related theme in imagery

I hope that you have made a commitment to act on your general flexible/non-extreme attitudes. Assuming that you have, your basic task is for you to face up to threats posed to your relationship with your partner from another person and to uncertainty about the whereabouts, behaviour, thoughts and feelings of your partner, and to learn to think flexibly/non-extremely about it.

Up to this point, you have worked at a general level with respect to your unhealthy jealousy-related theme, dealing with the general rigid/extreme attitudes that account for your unhealthy jealousy and developing your alternative general flexible/non-extreme attitudes. However, when you come to apply your general flexible/non-extreme attitudes in dealing with threats posed to your relationship with your partner from another person and to uncertainty about the whereabouts, behaviour, thoughts and feelings of your partner, you need to bear in mind one important point. Since you make yourself unhealthily jealous about specific instances of this threat (actual or imagined) and related uncertainty, you need to deal with these by rehearsing specific variants of your general flexible/non-extreme attitudes.

While the best way to do this is in specific threat- and uncertainty-related situations, you may derive benefit by using imagery first. If this is the case, you need to do the following:

⊙ Imagine a specific situation in which you felt or may feel unhealthily jealous about a threat being posed to your relationship with your partner from another person or related to uncertainty about the whereabouts, behaviour, thoughts and feelings of your partner and focus, in your mind's eye, on what you felt most unhealthily jealous about (i.e., your 'A').

⊙ Focus on this 'A' while rehearsing a specific flexible/non-extreme attitude relevant to the situation. As you do this, try to make yourself feel healthily jealous, rather than unhealthily jealous.

- Then see yourself acting in ways consistent with your flexible/non-extreme attitude, e.g., expressing your concern to your partner and listening with an open mind to what he or she has to say in response.

- Recognise that some of your post-rigid/extreme-attitude thinking may be distorted. Respond to it without getting bogged down doing so. Accept the presence of any remaining distorted thoughts without engaging with them.

- Repeat the above steps until you feel sufficiently ready to put this sequence into practice in your life.

If you find that facing your unhealthily jealousy-related adversity at 'A', in your mind's eye, is too much for you, use the 'challenging, but not overwhelming' principle that I introduced in Chapter 2 (see p. 33). This means that, instead of imagining yourself facing a threat to your relationship or an instance of uncertainty about your partner's whereabouts that you find 'overwhelming' at the present time, choose a similar unhealthy jealousy-related 'A' that you would find 'challenging, but not overwhelming'. Then employ the same steps that I have outlined above. Work in this way with modified unhealthy jealousy-related 'A's' until you find your original one 'challenging, but not overwhelming' and then use the steps again.

Step 9: Act in ways that are consistent with your general flexible/non-extreme attitude

As I mentioned earlier, when you experience the emotional problem of unhealthy jealousy and the thoughts that accompany it, you will also experience a strong urge to act on them. If you do, you will serve only to strengthen the rigid/extreme attitudes that underpin such behaviour. So, after you have examined your rigid/extreme and flexible/non-extreme attitudes in the way I suggested above and committed yourself to strengthening your conviction in your flexible/non-extreme attitudes, it is very important that you act in ways that will do this and to refrain from acting in ways that will do the opposite.

This is perhaps the most important principle involved in dealing effectively with unhealthy jealousy. I have seen many people in my practice who have had ineffective therapy where the focus was on helping them to identify the childhood roots of these feelings. I am not against this practice, but the reason such therapy often fails is that, while the person is engaged in such an exploration, they are acting, in the present, in ways that stem from their rigid/extreme attitudes and serve only to reinforce these attitudes.

So, it is crucial that you act according to the behavioural goals that you identified in Step 4 and accept that, while you do so, you will still have the urge to act and think in unhealthy ways. Accept that this is an almost inevitable and natural part of the change process and that these unhealthy urges and thoughts will eventually subside if you do not engage with them. I stress that this is difficult, but if you are clear about what you need to do and act accordingly, you will stack the odds in favour of, rather than against, dealing effectively with your unhealthy jealousy.

Step 10: Capitalise on what you have learned

When you have faced a situation in which you experienced unhealthy jealousy and dealt with it as best you could, it is important that you reflect on what you did and what you learned. In particular, if you were able to face the situation, and rehearse your specific flexible/non-extreme attitudes until you felt healthy jealousy, ask yourself how you can capitalise on what you achieved. If you experienced any problems, respond to the following questions:

- Did I face the situation and, if not, why not?
- Did I rehearse my flexible/non-extreme attitudes before, during or after facing the situation and, if not, why not?
- Did I execute my plan to face the situation and, if not, why not?
- Did I engage with post-rigid/extreme attitude distorted thinking and, if so, why?

Reflect on your experience and put into practice what you have learned the next time you face a situation in which someone poses a threat to your relationship or where a threat is posed to you by uncertainty concerning your partner's whereabouts, behaviour or thinking in the context of the first threat.

Step 11: Generalise your learning

Once you have dealt with your unhealthy jealousy in a specific situation by holding the relevant specific version of your general flexible/non-extreme attitude and by acting and thinking in ways that are consistent with it, you can generalise this learning to situations defined by your unhealthy jealousy-based theme.

Donald was particularly prone to unhealthy jealousy about women he was going out with. Thus:

- Donald assessed the three components of his unhealthy jealousy response and set goals with respect to all three components.

- He identified his relevant general rigid/extreme attitudes regarding what he saw as threats to his relationship with his current girlfriend (i.e., 'I must be the only person that my girlfriend is attracted to and, if I'm not, I am less worthy than my rival') and uncertainty about her whereabouts ('I must know where my girlfriend is and what she is doing at all times and I can't bear not knowing this') that underpinned his unhealthy jealousy response. He then identified his alternative general flexible/non-extreme attitudes towards the third person threat (i.e., 'I would like to be the only person that my girlfriend is attracted to, but I don't have to be. If I'm not, I am not less worthy than my rival. I am equal in worth to him') and the uncertainty threat (i.e., 'I would like to know where my girlfriend is and what she is doing at all times, but I do not need to know this. I can bear not knowing this even though it is difficult and it is worth it to me to do so') that underpinned his healthy jealousy response.

- He examined both elements of his general rigid/extreme attitudes and his general flexible/non-extreme attitudes until he clearly saw that the former were false, made no sense and were detrimental to him, and that the latter were true, sensible and healthy.

- He acted on shortened versions of his flexible/non-extreme attitudes in specific situations and did not keep checking on his girlfriend, either when she was talking to other men or when he did not know where she was or what she was doing. Instead, he acted as if he trusted her to be faithful to him, even though she might find other men attractive. However, he did disclose his feelings of displeasure towards her if it was clear that she was being overly flirtatious towards other men at social gatherings.

- As he acted on his flexible/non-extreme attitudes, he tolerated the discomfort that he felt and accepted that some of his distorted and skewed negative thinking would still be in his mind as he did so. He let such thinking be without engaging with it, suppressing it or distracting himself from it.

As this section shows, you can generalise what you learn about dealing with unhealthy jealousy from situation to situation as defined by your unhealthy jealousy-based inference.

USING REBT'S ABCD FORM TO DEAL WITH SPECIFIC EXAMPLES OF YOUR UNHEALTHY JEALOUSY

This chapter is mainly geared to help you deal with your unhealthy jealousy in general terms. However, you can also use this material to address specific examples of your unhealthy jealousy. I have developed a self-help form to provide the structure to assist you in this regard. It is called the ABCD form and it appears with instructions in Appendix 6.

OTHER IMPORTANT ISSUES IN DEALING WITH UNHEALTHY JEALOUSY

In the above section, I outlined an 11-step programme to deal with unhealthy jealousy. In this section, I discuss some other important issues that may be relevant to you in your work to become less prone to this emotional problem. If you want to, you can incorporate them as additional steps in the above step-by-step guide at points relevant to you.

Dealing with your safety-seeking measures to avoid unhealthy jealousy

I mentioned in Chapter 2 that people use safety-seeking measures to protect themselves from threat. You may use similar measures to protect yourself from feeling unhealthy jealousy. Here is how this works from your perspective. You reason that, since you feel unhealthy jealousy about 'third person' and 'uncertainty' threats to your relationship with your partner, you will take steps to avoid unhealthy jealousy. This involves you ensuring that your partner does not interact with potential rivals and that you know where your partner is and what he or she is doing.

However, this stance and the reasoning that leads you to take it are flawed and will serve only to perpetuate your tendency to feel unhealthy jealousy. This is due to the fact that your unhealthy jealousy is not based on 'third person' and 'uncertainty' threats to your relationship, but on your rigid/extreme attitudes towards such threats. So, if you want to deal effectively with unhealthy jealousy, you need to do the following:

- Do not attempt to prevent your partner from interacting with potential rivals.

- Do not keep tabs on your partner. Allow your partner to do what they want without you knowing exactly where your partner is, what they are doing and with whom they are interacting.

- If you actually face threats to your relationship as a result, deal with these by bringing to such situations appropriate specific versions of your general flexible/non-extreme attitudes so that you feel healthily jealous and not unhealthy jealousy about these episodes. Also, act and think in ways that are consistent with these specific flexible/non-extreme attitudes as far as you can.

Why you feel unhealthy jealousy much of the time and how to deal with this

If you are particularly prone to unhealthy jealousy, you hold the following attitude, which I call a 'chronic unhealthy jealousy-based general rigid/extreme attitude':

- 'I must know for sure that my relationship is not under threat and I can't bear not knowing this. If I don't have such certainty, then my relationship is under threat, and I will lose my partner because I am not good enough to hold any partner in the face of such threat.'

As you can see, this attitude has a number of elements:

- It relates to the threat of uncertainty and you finding not knowing unbearable.

⊚ It relates to the threat to your relationship and the self-devaluation attitude you implicitly hold.

Holding this attitude, you will do the following:

⊚ You will assume that uncertainty means that your relationship is under threat. Thus, you will see threat in ordinary exchanges between your partner and others where none objectively exists.

⊚ You will think that you will lose out to any rival because they have more to offer your partner than you do.

⊚ You will focus on past relationships where you thought your partner was unfaithful to you.

⊚ You will scan your current relationship hoping not to find, but certain that you will find, evidence that your partner is interested in someone else and is making plans to leave you. If there is any ambiguity about this, you will err on the side of threat to and loss of your relationship.

⊚ You will employ all the thinking and behavioural strategies that you use to keep yourself safe from threat. This serves only to strengthen your conviction that you are under threat.

How to deal with chronic unhealthy jealousy

In order to deal with this chronic sense of unhealthy jealousy, you need to develop and apply an alternative general flexible/non-extreme attitude that protects you from such unhealthy jealousy.

⊚ 'I would like to know for sure that my relationship is not under threat, but, although it is a struggle, I can bear not knowing this and it is worth it to me to do so. If I don't have such certainty, it does not follow that my relationship is under threat, unless there is objective evidence that it is. If there is such a threat, then it does not follow that I will lose my partner. I am fallible and good enough to hold any partner in the face of such threat.'

When you hold this attitude and there exists objective evidence that your relationship is under threat, you will feel healthy jealousy rather than unhealthy jealousy because you will be processing this with a specific flexible/non-extreme attitude.

In addition, this attitude will help you to:

- revisit your past and see that past partners were more trustworthy than you thought at the time;

- see that your current partner is more trustworthy than you think when you hold your set of specific and general rigid/extreme attitudes; and

- see that any future partners will be trustworthy unless you find objective evidence to the contrary.

How to examine the accuracy of your unhealthy jealousy-related inference, if necessary

If you are still unsure whether a threat exists to your relationship or not, answer one or more of the following questions:

- How valid is my inference that there is a threat to my relationship?

- Would an objective jury agree that there is a threat to my relationship? If not, what would the jury's verdict be?

- Is my inference that there is a threat to my relationship realistic? If not, what is a more realistic inference?

- If I asked someone whom I could trust to give me an objective opinion about my inference that there is a threat to my relationship, what would that person say to me and why? What inference would this person encourage me to make instead?

- If a friend had told me that they had made the same inference about them facing a threat to their relationship, what would I say to this friend about the validity of their inference and why? What inference would I encourage this friend to make instead?

Assessing and dealing with emotional problems about unhealthy jealousy

In previous chapters, I discussed the concept of meta-disturbance (literally disturbance about disturbance). It is important to assess carefully the nature of this meta-disturbance about unhealthy jealousy before you can best deal with it.

The best way to start dealing with the assessment of any emotional problems you might have about unhealthy jealousy is to ask yourself the question: 'How do I feel about my feeling of unhealthy jealousy?' The most common emotional problems that people have about unhealthy jealousy are as follows: anxiety, depression, unhealthy regret, shame and unhealthy self-anger. I refer you to the relevant chapters on these emotional problems in this book for help on how to deal with meta-emotional problems about unhealthy jealousy.

Developing and rehearsing healthy jealousy-based world views

People develop views of the world as it relates to them that make it more or less likely that they will experience UNEs. The world views that render you vulnerable to unhealthy jealousy do so in a similar way to the chronic unhealthy jealousy-based general rigid/extreme attitude discussed above (i.e., 'I must know for sure that my relationship is not under threat and I can't stand not knowing this. If I don't have such certainty then my relationship is under threat and I will lose my partner because I am not good enough to hold any partner in the face of such threat') by making you focus unduly on times when you have, are or will face threats to your relationship. However, these unhealthy jealousy-based world views have this effect on you much more widely.

It is important that you develop realistic views of the world that will help you to deal with unhealthy jealousy and experience healthy jealousy instead. In Table 9.1, you will find an illustrative list of such world views rather than an exhaustive one, so you can get an idea of what I mean, which will enable you to develop your own. In Table 9.1, I first describe a world view that renders you vulnerable to unhealthy jealousy and then I give its healthy alternative. You will see that the former views are characterised by a conception of your partners as being basically untrustworthy and potential rivals as being basically predatory. In the latter views, a more benign, balanced, but realistic picture of others is revealed and thus a healthier response to the possible existence of relationship threat can be expected.

If you hold flexible/non-extreme attitudes that are consistent with the views of the world listed on the right-hand side of Table 9.1, and if you

Table 9.1 World views that render you vulnerable to unhealthy jealousy and help you to deal with unhealthy jealousy

Views of the world that render you vulnerable to unhealthy jealousy	Views of the world that help you deal with unhealthy jealousy
◉ My partners are ultimately untrustworthy	◉ Some of my partners may be untrustworthy, but most will probably be trustworthy
◉ My partners will ultimately leave me	◉ Some of my partners may leave me, but others won't. However, I may drive away people in this last group through my jealous behaviour
◉ If I trust someone, they will make a fool of me. So, I need to always be on my guard	◉ If I trust someone, it is possible that the person may betray my trust, but it is also possible that they won't. If they do, they can't make a fool out of me – only I can do this with my rigid and self-devaluation attitudes towards their behaviour
◉ Not knowing what my partner is feeling, thinking and doing is very dangerous	◉ Not knowing what my partner is feeling, thinking and doing is not inherently dangerous
◉ Every attractive person is my rival	◉ Some attractive people may be my rivals, but most won't be
◉ Attractive people are predatory and will seek to displace me in the affections of my partner	◉ A few attractive people are predatory and will seek to displace me in the affections of my partner, but most will not

act and think in ways that are, in turn, consistent with these flexible/non-extreme attitudes, you will become less prone to unhealthy jealousy.

In Chapter 10, I discuss unhealthy envy and how to deal with it.

NOTE

1 As I have mentioned before, we don't have agreed terms for HNEs. Therefore, if you don't resonate with the term 'healthy jealousy', use a term that makes more sense to you.

Dealing with unhealthy envy

In this chapter, I begin by presenting REBT's way of understanding unhealthy envy and then address how to deal with this emotional problem.

UNDERSTANDING UNHEALTHY ENVY

In understanding unhealthy envy, we need to know what we tend to make ourselves feel unhealthily envious about (i.e., its major inference themes), what attitudes we hold, how we act or tend to act, and how we think when we are unhealthily envious.

Major inference theme in unhealthy envy

The major theme in relation to your personal domain that is implicated in unhealthy envy is that someone has something that you prize, but don't have. In unhealthy envy, your focus may be on the object,[1] that is you think you really want the object for its own sake (I call this object-focused unhealthy envy), or on the person who has the object, i.e., you prize the object only because the particular person has it (I call this person-focused unhealthy envy). The common denominator in these different types of envy is that you consider yourself to be in a state of deprivation.

Rigid/extreme attitudes

As I explained in Chapter 1, according to REBT, inferences on their own do not account for emotional problems. It is possible, therefore, for you to make the same inference as listed above and feel healthy envy and not unhealthy envy.[2] In order for you to feel unhealthy envy, you have to hold a rigid attitude and one or more extreme attitudes. While the rigid attitude is at the core of unhealthy envy, the extreme attitudes that are derived

DOI: 10.4324/9781003424307-10

from the rigid attitude often distinguish between whether you are experiencing unhealthy ego envy (where you devalue yourself) and unhealthy non-ego envy (where you 'awfulise', find the deprivation or inequality involved unbearable or devalue the other who is involved). You may, of course, experience both unhealthy ego envy and unhealthy non-ego envy in a given situation.

Behaviour associated with unhealthy envy

When you hold a rigid/extreme attitude towards someone having something that you prize, but don't have, you will act or tend to act in a number of ways, the most common of which are as follows:

◉ You disparage verbally the person who has the desired possession to others.

◉ You disparage verbally the desired possession to others.

◉ If you had the chance, you would take away the desired possession from the other (either so that you will have it or so that the other is deprived of it).

◉ If you had the chance, you would spoil or destroy the desired possession so that the other person does not have it.

Thinking associated with unhealthy envy

When you hold a rigid/extreme attitude towards someone having something that you prize, but don't have, you will tend to think in a number of ways. Remember what I said in Chapter 1: the thinking that accompanies your unhealthy envy is the result of your inference being processed by your rigid/extreme attitude and therefore it is likely to contain a number of thinking errors that I present in Appendix 1. I list the main features of this post-rigid/extreme attitude unhealthy envy-based thinking below:

◉ You tend to denigrate in your mind the value of the desired possession and/or the person who possesses it.

◉ You try to convince yourself that you are happy with your possessions (although you are not).

- You think about how to acquire the desired possession regardless of its usefulness.

- You think about how to deprive the other person of the desired possession.

- You think about how to spoil or destroy the other's desired possession.

As you can see, such thinking deepens the sense of deprivation that you experience and exaggerates the inequality that there is between you and the other person or persons involved. Once again, such thinking may be in words or in mental images.

HOW TO DEAL WITH UNHEALTHY ENVY

If you are prone to unhealthy envy, you tend to experience this emotional problem in a variety of different settings and in response to a variety of situations where someone has something that you prize, but don't have. Here is how to deal with unhealthy envy so that you become less prone to it.

Step 1: Identify reasons why unhealthy envy is a problem for you and why you want to change

While unhealthy envy is generally regarded as an emotional problem, it is useful for you to spell out reasons why unhealthy envy is a problem for you and why you want to change. I suggest that you keep a written list of these reasons and refer to it as needed as a reminder of why you are engaged in a self-help programme. I discuss the healthy alternative to unhealthy envy in Step 4.

What makes it harder for you to admit that you have an envy problem is that it is often an 'ugly' emotion (in that you seek to destroy or spoil what others have), you often feel ashamed of the malevolence that often accompanies unhealthy envy and thus, to cope with your shame, you deny having an envy problem. If you suspect that this is the case, I suggest that you deal with your shame about your envy first (see Chapter 6) and then come back to dealing with your unhealthy envy once you are disappointed, but not ashamed, about your unhealthy envy response.

Step 2: Take responsibility for your unhealthy envy

In REBT, we argue that people or things do not make you unhealthily envious; rather you create these feelings by the rigid/extreme attitudes that you hold towards such people and things. You may object that this involves you blaming yourself for creating your feelings of unhealthy envy, but this objection is based on a misconception. It assumes that taking responsibility for creating your unhealthy envy is synonymous with self-blame. In truth, responsibility means that you take ownership for the rigid/extreme attitudes that underpin your unhealthy envy while accepting yourself for doing so. Blame, on the other hand, means that you regard yourself as being bad for creating your own unhealthy envy.

Step 3: Identify the themes about which you tend to feel unhealthy envy

The best way of identifying what you tend to feel unhealthy envy about is to understand the major theme associated with unhealthy envy and how this theme is manifest with respect to your personal domain. As I outlined, the major theme in unhealthy envy is when someone else has something that you prize, but don't have. It is also important that you distinguish between unhealthy envy that is mainly object focused (in which case keep a list of the objects that you tend to covet) or person focused (in which case keep a list of the people about whom you tend to be envious).

Step 4: Identify the three components of your unhealthy envy response and set goals with respect to each component

The next step is for you to list the three elements of your unhealthy envy response in the face of each of the relevant themes listed above.

Identify the three components of your unhealthy envy response

I use the term 'unhealthy envy response' to describe the three main components that make up this response. The three components of your unhealthy envy response are the emotional, behavioural and thinking components.

Emotional component

The emotional component here is, of course, unhealthy envy.

Behavioural component

The behavioural component concerns overt behaviour or action tendencies that you engage in or 'feel like' engaging in when you feel unhealthy envy. Consult the list that I provided to help you identify your behaviour associated with each relevant theme when you feel unhealthy envy (see p. 188).

Thinking component

The thinking component associated with unhealthy envy is listed on pp. 188–189. Again, these may be in words or in mental pictures. Consult this list if necessary.

Set goals with respect to each of the three components

You need to set goals so that you know what you are striving for when you deal effectively with unhealthy envy. The three goals are emotional, behavioural and thinking goals.

Emotional goal

Your emotional goal is healthy envy rather than unhealthy envy (or whatever synonym you prefer to the term 'healthy envy'). Healthy envy is an HNE, which is an appropriate response to someone having something that you prize, but don't have. It helps you to think objectively about the situation and your response to it and helps you to move on with your life rather than get stuck or bogged down.

Behavioural goal

Your behavioural goal should reflect actions that are based on healthy envy rather than unhealthy envy. The following are the most common behaviours associated with healthy envy. You may wish to compare these behaviours with those associated with unhealthy envy that I presented on p. 188.

⊚ You strive to obtain the desired possession if it is truly what you want.

Thinking goal

As well as setting behavioural goals related to the feeling of healthy envy about a situation where someone has something that you want but lack, it is important that you set thinking goals associated with this emotion. The following are the most common forms of thinking associated with healthy envy rather than unhealthy envy. Again, you may wish to compare these forms of thinking with those associated with unhealthy envy that I presented on pp. 188–189.

⊚ You honestly admit to yourself that you desire the desired possession.

⊚ You are honest with yourself if you are not happy with your possessions, rather than defensively trying to convince yourself that you are happy with them when you are not.

⊚ You think about how to obtain the desired possession because you desire it for healthy reasons.

⊚ You can allow the other person to have and enjoy the desired possession without denigrating that person or the possession.

As the above list shows, the dominant feature of thinking associated with healthy envy is that it is realistic and balanced. Please remember that such thinking may be in words or in mental pictures.

Step 5: Recognise that your symptoms of unhealthy envy are evidence of disturbance and not necessarily that you truly desire the prized object that the other person has, but you don't

Once you have identified your unhealthily envious response and its healthy alternative, it is important that you realise one important point. If you feel envious a lot, your feelings and the thoughts that accompany them are most likely to be evidence that you have an envy problem rather than proof that you truly desire what the other has that you don't.

When you think that you really want something that others have that you don't because you have envious feelings and envious thoughts, you are again succumbing to the two thinking errors known as emotional reasoning and cognitive reasoning. In emotional reasoning, you assume that, because you feel envious, that is evidence that you truly want the prized object. In cognitive reasoning, you think that your envious thoughts are proof that again your desire is for the object itself and not to make equal what in your eyes is an unequal situation (where someone has what you prize, but don't have).

If your unhealthy envy is chronic, when you have envious feelings and thoughts, your task is to remind yourself that these are, in all probability, signs that you need to identify and deal with the rigid/extreme attitudes that underpin your unhealthy envy response rather than to act on them. You may well find this difficult, because, when you have envious feelings and thoughts, you will also experience an urge to act on them. Refraining from doing so will go against the grain and will thus be uncomfortable, but, if you do so, you will put yourself in the position of dealing effectively with your unhealthy envy. If you don't, you will maintain this emotional problem.

Step 6: Identify your general rigid/extreme attitudes and alternative general flexible/ non-extreme attitudes

A general rigid/extreme attitude leading to your unhealthy envy response is a rigid/extreme attitude that you hold across situations defined by the major theme: someone has something that you prize, but don't have. Remember that your unhealthy envy can be object focused or person focused (see p. 187 for how to distinguish between the two). In addition, your unhealthy envy may relate to the ego part or the non-ego part of your personal domain. The flexible/non-extreme alternative to this attitude, which will also be general in nature, will account for your healthy envy response.

Identify your general rigid/extreme attitudes

When you identify a general rigid/extreme attitude, you take a common unhealthy envy-related theme (see above) and add to this a general rigid attitude and the main extreme attitude that is derived from the rigid attitude. In unhealthy envy, your main extreme attitude will be either an unbearability attitude or a self-devaluation attitude.

Let me provide examples of the rigid/extreme attitudes associated with each of the four types of unhealthy envy:

- Object-focused unhealthy ego envy:

  'I must have the latest gadgets that some of my friends have and, if I don't have them, I am useless.'

- Object-focused unhealthy non-ego envy:

  'I must have the latest gadgets that some of my friends have and I can't bear the deprivation of not having them.'

- Person-focused unhealthy ego envy:

  'I must have what my younger sisters have and, if I don't, then they are better than me.'

- Person-focused unhealthy non-ego envy:

  'I must have what my younger sisters have and I can't bear the inequality of not having what they have.'

Identify your alternative general flexible/non-extreme attitudes

When you identify your alternative general flexible/non-extreme attitude, you take the same common theme and add to this a general flexible attitude and a general discomfort tolerance attitude or a general self-acceptance attitude. For example:

- Object-focused healthy ego envy:

  'I would like to have the latest gadgets that some of my friends have, but it is not necessary that I have them. If I don't have them, that is unfortunate, but it does not prove that I am useless. I am a unique, unrateable, fallible human being whether or not I have these gadgets.'

- Object-focused healthy non-ego envy:

  'I would like to have the latest gadgets that some of my friends have, but it is not necessary that I have them. If I don't have them, it would be a struggle for me to bear the deprivation, but I can do so, it would be worth it to me to do so and I am worth doing it for.'

◉ Person-focused healthy ego envy:

'I would like to have what my younger sisters have, but I don't have to have them. If I don't, that would be bad, but it would not prove that they are better than me. I am equal to them even though they may have more than me.'

◉ Person-focused healthy non-ego envy:

'I would like to have what my younger sisters have, but I don't have to have them. It would be hard for me to bear the resultant inequality, but I can do so, it would be worth it to me to do so and I am worth doing it for.'

Step 7: Examine your general attitudes

I recommended in previous chapters that you first examine together your general rigid attitude and its general flexible attitude alternative and then examine together your general extreme attitude and its general non-extreme attitude alternative.

Examine your general rigid attitude and its general flexible attitude alternative

First, take your general rigid attitude and its general flexible attitude alternative and write them down next to one another on a sheet of paper. Then ask yourself:

◉ Which is true and which is false?

◉ Which is sensible logically and which does not make sense?

◉ Which has largely constructive results and which has largely unconstructive results?

Write down your answer to each of these questions on your piece of paper, giving reasons for each answer. Consult Appendix 2 for help with the answers to these questions, which you need to adapt and apply to the attitudes you are examining.

Examine your general extreme attitude and its general non-extreme attitude alternative

Next, take your general extreme attitude and its general non-extreme attitude alternative and again write them down next to one another on a sheet of paper. Then, ask yourself the same three questions that you used with your general rigid attitude and its general flexible attitude alternative. Again, write down your answer to each of these questions on your piece of paper, giving reasons for each answer. I suggest that you consult Appendix 3 (for help with examining awfulising attitudes and non-awfulising attitudes), Appendix 4 (for help with examining unbearability attitudes and bearability attitudes) and Appendix 5 (for help with examining devaluation attitudes and unconditional acceptance attitudes). Again, you need to adapt and apply these arguments to the attitudes you are examining.

You should now be ready to commit to acting and thinking in ways consistent with your general flexible/non-extreme attitude.

Step 8: Face your unhealthy envy-related theme in imagery

I hope that you have made a commitment to act on your general flexible/non-extreme attitudes (i.e., flexible attitude and unconditional self-acceptance attitude). Assuming that you have, your basic task is to face up to someone having something that you prize, but don't have, and to learn to think flexibly and in a non-extreme way about it.

Up to this point, you have worked at a general level with respect to your unhealthy envy-related theme, dealing with the general rigid/extreme attitudes that account for your unhealthy envy and developing your alternative general flexible/non-extreme attitudes. However, when you come to apply your general flexible/non-extreme attitudes in dealing with someone having something that you prize, but don't have, you need to bear in mind one important point. Since you make yourself unhealthily envious about specific events (actual or imagined) where someone has something that you prize, but do not have, you need to deal with these events by rehearsing specific variants of your general flexible/non-extreme attitudes.

While the best way to do this is in specific situations where someone has something that you prize, but don't have, you may derive benefit by using imagery first. If this is the case, you need to do the following:

- Imagine a specific situation in which you felt or may feel unhealthily envious about someone having something that you prize, but don't have, and focus, in your mind's eye, on what you felt most unhealthily envious about (i.e., your 'A' or adversity).

- Focus on this 'A' while rehearsing a specific flexible/non-extreme attitude relevant to the situation. As you do this, try to make yourself feel healthily envious, rather than unhealthily envious.

- Then see yourself acting in ways consistent with your flexible/non-extreme attitude, such as expressing admiration for rather than denigrating the person or object concerned.

- Recognise that some of your post-rigid/extreme-attitude thinking may be distorted. Respond to it without getting bogged down doing so. Accept the presence of any remaining distorted thoughts without engaging with them.

- Repeat the above steps until you feel sufficiently ready to put this sequence into practice in your life.

If you find that facing your unhealthy envy-related adversity at 'A', in your mind's eye, is too much for you, use the 'challenging, but not overwhelming' principle that I introduced in Chapter 2 (see p. 33). This means that, instead of imagining yourself facing someone having something that you prize, but don't have, that you find 'overwhelming' at the present time, choose a similar unhealthy related 'A' that you would find 'challenging, but not overwhelming'. Then employ the same steps that I have outlined above. Work in this way with modified unhealthy envy-related 'A's' until you find your original one 'challenging, but not overwhelming' and then use the steps again.

Step 9: Act in ways that are consistent with your general flexible/non-extreme attitude

As I mentioned earlier, when you experience the emotional problem of unhealthy envy and the thoughts that accompany it, you will also experience a strong urge to act on them. If you do, you will serve only to strengthen the rigid/extreme attitudes that underpin such behaviour. So, after you have examined your rigid/extreme and flexible/non-extreme attitudes in the way I suggested above and committed yourself to strengthening your conviction in your flexible/non-extreme attitudes, it is very important that you act in ways that will do this and refrain from acting in ways that will do the opposite.

So, it is crucial that you act according to the behavioural goals that you identified in Step 3 and accept that, while you do so, you will still have the urge to act and think in unhealthy ways. Accept that this is an almost inevitable and natural part of the change process and these unhealthy urges and thoughts will eventually subside if you do not engage with them. I stress that this is difficult, but if you are clear about what you need to do and act accordingly, you will stack the odds in favour of, rather than against, you dealing effectively with your unhealthy envy.

Step 10: Capitalise on what you have learned

When you have faced a situation in which you experienced unhealthy envy and dealt with it as best you could, it is important that you reflect on what you did and what you learned. In particular, if you were able to face the situation, and rehearse your specific flexible/non-extreme attitudes until you felt healthy envy, ask yourself how you can capitalise on what you achieved. If you experienced any problems, respond to the following questions:

- Did I face the situation and, if not, why not?

- Did I rehearse my flexible/non-extreme attitudes before, during or after facing the situation and, if not, why not?

- Did I execute my plan to face the situation and, if not, why not?

- Did I engage with post-rigid/extreme attitude distorted thinking and, if so, why?

Reflect on your experience and put into practice what you have learned the next time you face a situation in which someone has something that you prize, but lack.

Step 11: Generalise your learning

Once you have dealt with your unhealthy envy in a specific situation by holding the relevant specific version of your general flexible/non-extreme attitude and by acting and thinking in ways that are consistent with it, you can generalise this learning to situations defined by your unhealthy envy-based theme.

Virginia was particularly prone to person-focused unhealthy ego envy with respect to her friends' boyfriends. She did not have a boyfriend of her own and, to prove that she was lovable, she flirted with their boyfriends and encouraged them to make passes at her. When they did, she took that as proof that she was lovable and rebuffed their advances. In helping herself deal with this type of unhealthy envy, she did the following:

- Virginia assessed the three components of her unhealthy envy response and set goals with respect to all three components.

- She identified her relevant general rigid/extreme attitude regarding her envy-related theme (i.e., 'I must have what my friends have and I am less lovable than them if I don't') that underpinned her unhealthy envy response. She then identified her alternative general flexible/non-extreme attitude (i.e., 'I would like to have what my friends have, but I don't have to have it. It is frustrating when I don't have it, but it does not prove that I am less lovable than them. We are equal in lovability even if we are unequal in that they have what I want') that underpinned her healthy envy response.

- She examined her general rigid/extreme attitude and her general flexible/non-extreme attitude until she clearly saw that the former were false, made no sense and were detrimental to her, and that the latter were true, sensible and healthy.

- She acted on shortened versions of her flexible/non-extreme attitudes in specific situations and had non-flirtatious conversations with her friends' boyfriends rather than encouraging them to make passes at her.

- As she acted on her flexible/non-extreme attitudes, she tolerated the discomfort that she felt and accepted that some of her distorted and skewed negative thinking would still be in her mind as she did so. She let such thinking be without engaging with it, suppressing it or distracting herself from it.

As this section shows, you can generalise what you learn about dealing with unhealthy envy from situation to situation as defined by your unhealthy envy-based inference.

USING REBT'S ABCD FORM TO DEAL WITH SPECIFIC EXAMPLES OF YOUR UNHEALTHY ENVY

This chapter is mainly geared to help you deal with your unhealthy envy in general terms. However, you can also use this material to address specific examples of your unhealthy envy. I have developed a self-help form to provide the structure to assist you in this regard. It is called the ABCD form and it appears with instructions in Appendix 6.

OTHER IMPORTANT ISSUES IN DEALING WITH UNHEALTHY ENVY

In the above section, I outlined an 11-step programme to deal with unhealthy envy. In this section, I discuss some other important issues that may be relevant to you in your work to become less prone to this emotional problem. If you want to, you can incorporate them as additional steps in the above step-by-step guide at points relevant to you.

Rethinking the place of objects in your life

In unhealthy envy, you think a certain way about the place of objects in your life.[3] In object-focused unhealthy ego envy, you tend to think that such objects, particularly when you don't have them, define your worth as a person. Thus, when you don't have what you prize and another person has it, you think that you are less worthy than you would be if you did have it. Ironically, however, were you to possess the object, your self-esteem might be raised, but this would be temporary and you would devalue yourself when you focused on something else that someone else had that you prized, but lacked. This clearly shows that the possession of prized objects does not solve your self-esteem problem; rather, it perpetuates the problem. Self-devaluation in the face of someone having something that you prize but lack is a psychological problem and can be solved only by psychological means. In REBT, we argue that unconditional self-acceptance is the most robust solution to self-esteem problems and I suggest that you review this flexible/non-extreme attitude in Appendix 5. I also discuss it in my book *How to Accept Yourself*

(Dryden, 1999). Basically, holding this attitude means that, while you may prize the object that someone else has that you don't have, its lack does not lessen your worth and your possession of it does not raise your worth. Your worth is fixed and is most healthily based on certain facts about you that do not change (i.e., your humanity, your fallibility, your uniqueness and your aliveness). It may be better if you possessed the object, but you are not better for having it. Interestingly, holding this flexible/non-extreme attitude helps you to determine how important the object really is to you, once you have stripped it of its power to determine your self-worth!

In object-focused non-ego unhealthy envy, you tend to think of prized objects that others have but you lack as 'must have' items that are necessary for your overall happiness rather than things that are desirable and may improve the quality of a restricted part of your life. Once you think that something is necessary, rather than desirable but not necessary, you overvalue it and often become obsessed by it. However, as in object-focused unhealthy ego envy, if you finally possess the object, your joy will be short-lived as you focus on something else that someone else has that you prize but lack. Again, the rigid and unbearability attitudes that underpin object-focused non-ego unhealthy envy represent the existence of a psychological problem that is perpetuated rather than solved by the possession of prized objects. Indeed, if you are prone to this type of unhealthy envy, it is very likely that you will have a large collection of discarded objects that you once saw as essential to your life. You discard such items as soon as you focus on another object that someone else has that you prize but lack. It is only when you adopt a set of flexible/non-extreme (flexible and bearability) attitudes that you will take a realistic position on the role of objects in your life and, in doing so, you will pursue only objects that will have enduring value for you.

Making healthy comparisons

As I have already shown you, in person-focused unhealthy envy your focus is on the person who has the object that you think you prize rather than on the object itself. I say 'think you prize' here because, in this type of unhealthy envy, should someone else with whom you are not in competition possess this object, you will not experience unhealthy envy. Thus, person-focused unhealthy envy involves competition and comparison.

The goal of flexible/non-extreme thinking is not to eradicate competition and comparison, but to maximise the chances that, when you are competitive and make comparisons, you do so healthily.

In person-focused unhealthy ego envy, you are making comparisons between yourself and another person with whom you feel competitive, and, if you lose out in the comparison, your self-esteem goes down. As in object-focused unhealthy ego envy, in its person-focused counterpart you adhere to the idea that you can rate a person and your rival has more worth than you if the other person has something that you think you prize but lack. To deal with this type of unhealthy envy, once again you need to develop an attitude of unconditional self-acceptance and realise that you and your rival are equal in worth and that this cannot be altered by the possession or non-possession of prized objects. Adopting this philosophy will help you determine whether you want the prized object for what it can offer you in that sphere of your life or whether you want it only because your rival has it.

In person-focused unhealthy non-ego envy, you make a similar comparison between yourself and your rival and you conclude that it is unfair when your rival has something that you think you prize but lack. The root of this type of unhealthy envy is in your rigid attitude that such unfairness must not exist in the first place or must be eradicated in the second place and that, if not, the continuing unfairness is intolerable. As a result, you seek to make things fair either by getting what you don't have or by spoiling what the other person has. This is quite clearly a psychological problem and cannot be solved by making things fair. It can be solved only by adopting a healthy flexible/non-extreme attitude towards unfairness. You do this by swallowing a bitter pill and seeing that, however undesirable, there is no law of the universe that decrees that unfairness (as expressed in situations where certain people with whom you are in competition have what you think you prize, but don't have) must not exist in the first place or must be eradicated in the second place. You also see that the ongoing existence of such unfairness is difficult to tolerate, but you can tolerate it and it is worth it to you to do so.

If you adopt this philosophy, you will be able to determine whether or not you want the prized object for its own sake and whether or not it will have any enduring value for you. You will also see that, while it may be unfair (to you) not having what certain others have, it is equally unfair (to others) not having what you have. You will come to see, therefore, that 'unfairness' is an inference and a matter of perspective rather than an objectively determined fact.

Why you feel unhealthy envy much of the time and how to deal with this

If you are particularly prone to unhealthy envy, you hold the following attitude, which I call a 'chronic unhealthy envy-based general rigid/extreme attitude':

⊙ 'I must have what I want and, if I don't have it, I am unworthy (or less worthy than those with whom I am in competition who do have it). It is also unfair when I don't have what I want when others have it and I must eradicate this unfairness and I can't bear it if I can't.'

As you can see, this attitude refers to both ego and non-ego aspects, since in my experience people who have a problem with chronic envy have problems with envy in both these realms of the personal domain.

Holding this attitude, you will do the following:

⊙ You will focus on what you don't have when others have it and will assign more importance to this than to what you have. When you focus on what you don't have, you will disturb yourself with a specific version of your general rigid/extreme attitude.

⊙ You will initially be pleased to get what you have previously prized but lacked, but you will soon lose interest in this because you have used the object to solve your psychological problem and it can never do that and you will soon become aware of something else that others have that you want, but don't have.

⊙ You will ignore all the things that you have previously prized, obtained and lost interest in, and continue to think that what you presently covet will solve your envy problem.

How to deal with chronic unhealthy envy

To deal with this chronic sense of unhealthy envy, you need to develop and apply an alternative general flexible/non-extreme attitude that protects you from such unhealthy envy.

⊙ 'I would like to have what I want, but I don't need to have it. If I don't get it, that would be unfortunate, but it would not prove that I am unworthy (or less worthy than those with whom I am in competition who do have it). My worth is fixed and is equal to the worth of others and that cannot change unless I refuse to acknowledge this fact. While it may be unfair when I don't have what I want when others have it, I don't have to eradicate this unfairness and, if I can't, that would be hard to bear, but I can do so, it would be in my healthy interests to do so and I am worth bearing it for.'

When you hold this attitude and there exists objective evidence that others have what you truly want, you will feel healthy envy rather than unhealthy envy because you will be processing this with a specific flexible/non-extreme attitude.

In addition, this attitude will help you to

- focus on and appreciate what you do have as well as acknowledge what you truly want that others have and you don't;

- see that your possessions have their place, but are not as important as you previously thought; and

- pursue what you don't have when it is likely to have lasting rather than transitory value for you and when it is not too time consuming to pursue it.

How to examine the strength of your desire for what others have that you prize, but don't have

When you operate according to a set of general and specific flexible/non-extreme attitudes with respect to what someone else has that you prize, but don't have, you should be able to gauge how important the desired object truly is to you. However, if you are still unsure that you really want what others have that you prize, but don't have, answer one or more of the following questions:

- Ask yourself how strong is your desire for the prized object?

- Ask yourself whether or not you would still want the object if getting it did not improve your self-esteem or make you feel better about life?

- If the other people who possess the desired object suddenly discarded it, would you still want it?

- Draw up a list of pros and cons for striving to get the object.

Assessing and dealing with emotional problems about unhealthy envy

In previous chapters, I discussed the concept of meta-disturbance (literally disturbance about disturbance). It is important to assess carefully the nature of this meta-disturbance about unhealthy envy before you can best deal with it.

The best way to start dealing with the assessment of any emotional problems you might have about unhealthy envy is to ask yourself the question: 'How do I feel about my feeling of unhealthy envy?' The most common emotional problems that people have about unhealthy envy are as follows: anxiety, depression, unhealthy regret, shame and unhealthy self-anger. I refer you to the relevant chapters on these emotional problems in this book for help in dealing with meta-emotional problems about unhealthy envy.

Developing and rehearsing healthy envy-based world views

People develop views of the world as it relates to them that make it more or less likely that they will experience UNEs. The world views that render you vulnerable to unhealthy envy do so in a similar way to the chronic unhealthy envy-based general rigid/extreme attitude discussed above (i.e., 'I must have what I want and, if I don't have it, I am unworthy (or less worthy than those with whom I am in competition who do have it). It is also unfair when I don't have what I want when others have it and I must eradicate this unfairness and I can't bear it if I can't') by making you focus unduly on not having that which you prize when others do have it. However, these unhealthy envy-based world views have this effect on you much more widely.

It is important that you develop realistic views of the world that will help you to deal with unhealthy envy and experience healthy envy instead. In Table 10.1, you will find an illustrative list of such world views rather than an exhaustive one, so you can get an idea of what I mean, which will enable you to develop your own. In Table 10.1, I first describe a world view that renders you vulnerable to unhealthy envy and then I give its healthy alternative. You will see that the former views are characterised by a conception of life where objects and possessions are seen as the source of happiness and a major determinant of personal worth. In the latter

Table 10.1 World views that render you vulnerable to unhealthy envy and help you to deal with unhealthy envy

Views of the world that render you vulnerable to unhealthy envy	Views of the world that help you deal with unhealthy envy
◉ My worth is measured by my possessions	◉ My worth is determined by my aliveness and not by my possessions
◉ If others with whom I am in competition have more than me, they are worthier than me	◉ If others with whom I am in competition have more than me, they have more than me, but we are of equal worth
◉ The more I have, the happier I will be	◉ My happiness is determined by my striving to achieve what I find personally meaningful and I am unlikely to find such meaning in possessions
◉ I can be happy only if I get the possessions that I want	◉ I can be happy even if I do not get the possessions that I want
◉ If someone has what I want, I really want it	◉ If someone has what I want, I may think I really want it, but that level of desire is coloured by my feelings of unhealthy envy
◉ It's unfair if others have what I don't have, but it is fair if I have what others don't have	◉ If it's unfair that others have what I don't have, it's unfair to others if they don't have what I have

views, a more balanced view of life is put forward in which objects and possessions are not the 'be all and end all' of life and personal worth. As a result, these latter views will help you deal more healthily with situations where others have what you prize but lack.

If you hold flexible/non-extreme attitudes that are consistent with the views of the world listed on the right-hand side of Table 10.1, and if you act and think in ways that are, in turn, consistent with these flexible/non-extreme attitudes, you will become less prone to unhealthy envy.

We have reached the end of this book. I hope you have found it instructive and valuable and I would appreciate any feedback c/o the publisher.

NOTES

1 I am using the word 'object' here very broadly to include anything that you prize.
2 As I have mentioned before, we don't have agreed terms for HNEs. Therefore, if you don't resonate with the term 'healthy envy', use a term that makes more sense to you.
3 Please remember that I am using the term 'objects' in this chapter to include anything that you prize.

References

Beck, A.T. (1976). *Cognitive Therapy and the Emotional Disorders*. New York: International Universities Press.

Burns, D. (1980). *Feeling Good: The New Mood Therapy*. New York: William Morrow.

Dryden, W. (1999). *How to Accept Yourself*. London: Sheldon.

Gilbert, P. (2009). *The Compassionate Mind: A New Approach to Life's Challenges*. London: Robinson.

Appendix 1

Descriptions, foundations and illustrations of thinking errors and their realistic and balanced alternatives

Descriptions of thinking errors and realistic and balanced alternatives	Illustrations*
Jumping to unwarranted conclusions Here, when something bad happens, you make a negative interpretation and treat this as a fact even though there is no definite evidence that convincingly supports your conclusions	⊙ 'Since they have seen me fail... [as I absolutely should not have done]... <u>they will view me as an incompetent worm'</u>
Sticking to the facts and testing out your hunches Here, when something bad happens, you stick to the facts and resolve to test out any negative interpretations you may make, which you view as hunches to be examined rather than as facts	⊙ 'Since they have seen me fail... [as I would have preferred not to do, but do not demand that I absolutely should not have done]... I am not sure how they will view me. <u>I think that some will think badly of me, others will be compassionate towards me and yet others may not have noticed or be neutral about my failure. I can always ask them, if I want to know'</u>
All-or-none thinking Here, you use non-overlapping black or white categories	⊙ 'If I fail at any important task... [as I must not do]... <u>I will only ever fail again'</u>
Multi-category thinking Here, you make use of a number of relevant categories	⊙ 'If I do fail at any important task... [as I would prefer not to do, but do not demand that I must not do]... <u>I may well both succeed and fail at important tasks in the future'</u>

Overgeneralising Here, when something bad happens, you make a generalisation from this experience that goes far beyond the data at hand	◉ '[My boss must like me]... If my boss does not like me, <u>it follows that nobody at work will like me</u>'
Making a realistic generalisation Here, when something goes wrong, you make a generalisation from this experience that is warranted by the data at hand	◉ '[I want my boss to like me, but my boss does not have to do so]... If my boss does not like me, <u>it does not follow that others at work may or may not like me</u>'
Focusing on the negative Here, you pick out a single negative detail and dwell on it exclusively so that your vision of all reality becomes darkened, like the drop of ink that discolours the entire glass of water	◉ 'As things are going wrong... [as they must not do and it is unbearable that they are]... <u>I can't see any good that is happening in my life</u>'
Focusing on the complexity of experiences Here, you focus on a negative detail, but integrate this detail into the complexity of positive, negative and neutral features of life	◉ 'As things are going wrong... [as I prefer they did not, but don't demand this. When they do go wrong, I can bear it]... <u>I can see that my life is made up of the good, the bad and the neutral</u>'
Disqualifying the positive Here, you reject positive experiences by insisting they 'don't count' for some reason or other, thus maintaining a negative view that cannot be contradicted by your everyday experiences	◉ '[I absolutely should not have done the foolish things that I have done]... When others compliment me on the good things I have done, <u>they are only being kind to me by seeming to forget those foolish things</u>'
Incorporating the positive into a complex view of your experiences Here, you accept positive experiences and locate these into the complexity of positive, negative and neutral features of life	◉ '[I would have preferred not to have done the foolish things that I have done, but that does not mean that I absolutely should not have done them]... When others compliment me on the good things I have done, <u>I can accept these compliments as being genuine even though I also did some foolish things, which the others may also have recognised</u>'

Mind reading Here, you arbitrarily conclude that someone is reacting negatively to you, and you don't bother to check this out. You regard your thought as a fact	⦿ 'I made some errors in my presentation... [that I absolutely should not have made]... and, <u>when I looked at my boss, I thought he was thinking how hopeless I was and therefore he did think this</u>'
Owning and checking one's thoughts about the reactions of others Here, you may think someone is reacting negatively to you, but you check it out with the other person rather than regarding your thought as fact	⦿ 'I made some errors in my presentation... [that I would have preferred not to have made, but that does not mean that I absolutely should not have made them]... and, when I looked at my boss, <u>I thought he was thinking that I was hopeless, but I quickly realised that this was my thought rather than his and resolved to ask him about this in the morning</u>'
Fortune telling Here, you anticipate that things will turn out badly, and you feel convinced that your prediction is an already established fact	⦿ 'Because I failed at this simple task... [which I absolutely should not have done]... <u>I think that I will get a very bad appraisal and thus this will happen</u>'
Owning and checking one's thoughts about what will happen in the future Here, you anticipate that things may turn out badly, but you regard that, as a prediction, that needs examining against the available data and is not an established fact	⦿ Because I failed at this simple task... [which I would have preferred not to have done, but I do not have to be immune to so doing]... <u>I may get a very bad appraisal, but this is unlikely since I have done far more good than bad at work during the last year</u>'

Always and never thinking Here, when something bad happens, you conclude that it will always happen and/ or the good alternative will never occur	⦿ 'Because my present conditions of living are not good... [and they are actually unbearable because they must be better than they are]... <u>it follows that they'll always be this way and I'll never have any happiness</u>'
Balanced thinking about the past, present and future Here, when something bad happens you recognise that, while it may happen again, it is not inevitable that it will and it is very unlikely that it will always occur. Also, you recognise that the good alternative may well occur in the future and that it is very unlikely that it will never happen	⦿ 'Because my present conditions of living are not good... [but they are bearable because they don't have to be better than they are]... <u>it does not follow that they will always be that way, and I can be happy again</u>'
Magnifying Here, when something bad happens, you exaggerate its negativity	⦿ 'I made a faux pas when introducing my new colleague... [which I absolutely should not have done and it's awful that I did so]... <u>and this will have a very negative effect on my career</u>'
Keeping things in realistic perspective Here, when something bad happens, you view it in its proper perspective	⦿ 'I made a faux pas when introducing my new colleague... [which I wish I had not done, but I do not have to be exempt from doing. It's bad that I did so, but hardly the end of the world]... <u>and, while people may remember it for a day or two, I doubt that it will have much lasting impact on my career</u>'

Minimising Here, you inappropriately shrink things until they appear tiny (your own desirable qualities or other people's imperfections)	◉ '[I must do outstandingly well and I am completely useless when I do not do so]... <u>When I have seemingly done reasonably well, this is the result of luck and anyone could have done this. Whereas, if another person had done the same thing, I would acknowledge their achievement</u>'
Using the same balanced perspective for self and others Here, when you do something good and/or others do something bad, you can recognise this kind of behaviour for what it is	◉ '[I want to do outstandingly well, but I do not have to do so. I am not useless when I do not do so]... When I or someone else has seemingly done reasonably well, <u>this may be the result</u> of luck, but it may be because I or they <u>fully deserved to do well</u>'
Emotional reasoning Here, you assume that your negative emotions necessarily reflect the way things really are: 'I feel it, therefore it must be true'	◉ 'Because I have performed so poorly... [as I absolutely should not have done]... <u>I feel like everybody will remember my poor performance and my strong feeling proves that they will</u>'
Sound reasoning based on thinking and feeling	◉ Because I have performed so poorly... [as I wish I had not done, but do not demand this]... <u>I think and feel that people will have different responses to my performance: some negative and nasty, some compassionate and empathic, and some neutral and this is probably the case</u>'

Personalising Here, when a negative event occurs involving you that you may or may not be primarily responsible for, you see yourself definitely as the cause of it	⦿ 'I am involved in a group presentation and things are not going well... [Since I am acting worse than I absolutely should act]... and the audience is laughing, <u>I am sure they are laughing only at me</u>'
Making a realistic attribution Here, when a negative event occurs involving you that you may or may not be primarily responsible for, you acknowledge that you may be the cause of it, but you don't assume that you definitely are. Rather, you view the event from the whole perspective before making an attribution of cause, which is likely to be realistic	⦿ 'I am involved in a group presentation and things are not going well... [Since I am acting worse than I would like, but do not demand, I must do]... and the audience is laughing, <u>I am not sure who or what they are laughing at and, indeed, some might be laughing with us and not at us</u>'

Note: * In these illustrations, the attitudes (rigid/extreme and flexible/non-extreme) are shown in square brackets and the thinking errors and realistic and balanced alternatives are underlined.

Appendix 2

Reasons why rigid attitudes are false, illogical and have largely unhealthy consequences and flexible attitudes are true, logical and have largely healthy consequences

Rigid attitude	Flexible attitude
A rigid attitude is false For such a demand to be true the demanded conditions would already have to exist when they do not. Or, as soon as you make a demand, these demanded conditions would have to come into existence. Both positions are clearly false or inconsistent with reality.	**A flexible attitude is true** A flexible attitude is true because its two component parts are true. You can prove that you have a particular desire and can provide reasons why you want what you want. You can also prove that you do not have to get what you desire.
A rigid attitude is illogical A rigid attitude is based on the same desire as a flexible one but is transformed as follows: ⦿ *'I prefer that x happens (or does not happen)... and therefore this absolutely must (or must not) happen.'* The first component ['I prefer that x happens (or does not happen...)'] is not rigid, but the second component ['... and therefore this absolutely must (or must not) happen'] is rigid. As such, a rigid attitude is illogical since one cannot logically derive something rigid from something that is not rigid.	**A flexible attitude is logical** A flexible attitude is logical since both parts are not rigid and thus the second component logically follows from the first. Thus, consider the following flexible attitude: ⦿ *'I prefer that x happens (or does not happen)... but this does not mean that it must (or must not) happen.'* The first component ['I prefer that x happens (or does not happen)'...] is not rigid, and the second component ['... but this does not mean that it must (or must not) happen'] is also not rigid. Thus, a flexible attitude is logical because it is comprised of two non-rigid parts connected together logically.

A rigid attitude has largely unhealthy consequences	A flexible attitude has largely healthy consequences
A rigid attitude has largely unhealthy consequences because it tends to lead to UNEs, unconstructive behaviour and highly distorted and biased subsequent thinking when the person is facing an adversity.	A flexible attitude has largely healthy consequences because it tends to lead to HNEs, constructive behaviour and realistic and balanced subsequent thinking when the person is facing an adversity.

Appendix 3

Reasons why awfulising attitudes are false, illogical and have largely unhealthy consequences and non-awfulising attitudes are true, logical and have largely healthy consequences

Awfulising attitude	Non-awfulising attitude
An awfulising attitude is false	**A non-awfulising attitude is true**
When you hold an awfulising attitude towards your adversity, this attitude is based on the following ideas:	When you hold a non-awfulising attitude towards your adversity. this attitude is based on the following ideas:
⊙ Nothing could be worse.	⊙ Things could always be worse.
⊙ The event in question is worse than 100 per cent bad.	⊙ The event in question is less than 100 per cent bad.
⊙ No good could possibly come from this bad event.	⊙ Good could come from this bad event.
⊙ You cannot transcend this experience. It is the end.	⊙ You can transcend this experience. It is not the end.
All four ideas are false and thus your awfulising attitude is false.	All four ideas are true and thus your non-awfulising attitude is true.

An awfulising attitude is illogical	A non-awfulising attitude is logical
An awfulising attitude is based on the same evaluation of badness as a non-awfulising attitude, but is transformed as follows:	A non-awfulising attitude is logical since both parts are non-rigid and thus the second component logically follows from the first. Thus, consider the following non-awfulising attitude:
⊚ *'It is bad if x happens (or does not happen)... and therefore it is awful if it does happen (or does not happen).'*	⊚ *'It is bad if x happens (or does not happen)... but it is not awful if it does happen (or does not happen).'*
The first component ['It is bad if x happens (or does not happen...)'] is non-extreme, but the second component ['... and therefore it is awful if it does (or does not) happen'] is extreme. As such, an awfulising attitude is illogical since one cannot logically derive something extreme from something that is non-extreme.	The first component ['It is bad if x happens (or does not happen)'...] is non-extreme and the second component ['... but it is not awful if it does happen (or does not happen)'] is also non-extreme. Thus, a non-awfulising attitude is logical because it is comprised of two non-extreme parts connected together logically.
An awfulising attitude has largely unhealthy consequences	**A non-awfulising attitude has largely healthy consequences**
An awfulising attitude has largely unhealthy consequences because it tends to lead to UNEs, unconstructive behaviour and highly distorted and biased subsequent thinking when the person is facing an adversity.	A non-awfulising attitude has largely healthy consequences because it tends to lead to HNEs, constructive behaviour and realistic and balanced subsequent thinking when the person is facing an adversity.

Appendix 4

Reasons why unbearability attitudes are false, illogical and have largely unhealthy consequences and bearability attitudes are true, logical and have largely healthy consequences

Unbearability attitude	Bearability attitude
An unbearability attitude is false	**A bearability attitude is true**
When you hold an unbearability attitude towards your adversity, this attitude is based on the following components, which are all false:	When you hold a bearability attitude towards your adversity, this attitude is based on the following components, which are all true:
⦿ I am unable to bear the adversity. ⦿ I will die or disintegrate if the adversity continues to exist. ⦿ I will lose the capacity to experience happiness if the adversity continues to exist.	⦿ I am able to bear the adversity. ⦿ I will struggle if the adversity discomfort continues to exist, but I will neither die nor disintegrate. ⦿ I will not lose the capacity to experience happiness if the adversity continues to exist, although this capacity will be temporarily diminished.
⦿ Even if I could bear it, the adversity is not worth bearing (even though it is). ⦿ Even if I could bear it, I am not worth bearing it for. ⦿ Even if I could bear it, I am not willing to bear it. ⦿ Even if I could bear it, I am not going to bear it.	⦿ The adversity is worth bearing (assuming it is). ⦿ I am worth bearing it for. ⦿ I am willing to bear the adversity. ⦿ I am going to bear the adversity.
All seven components are false and thus your unbearability attitude is false.	All seven components are true and thus your bearability is true.

Unbearability attitude	Bearability attitude
An unbearability attitude is illogical	**A bearability attitude is logical**
An unbearability attitude is based on the same sense of struggle as a discomfort tolerance attitude, but is transformed as follows:	A bearability attitude is logical since all parts are non-extreme and are logically connected with one another. Thus, consider the following bearability attitude:
◉ *'It would be difficult for me to bear it if x happens (or does not happen)... and therefore I could not bear it.'*	◉ *'It would be difficult for me to bear it if x happens (or does not happen)... but I could bear it. It would be worth bearing and I am worth bearing it for. I am willing to bear it and I am going to bear it.'*
The first component ['It would be difficult for me to bear it if x happens (or does not happen...)'] is non-extreme, but the second component ['... and therefore I could not bear it'] is extreme. As such, an unbearability attitude is illogical since one cannot logically derive something extreme from something that is non-extreme.	All six components of the bearability attitude are non-extreme. Thus, a bearability attitude is logical because it is comprised of six components that are all connected together logically.
An unbearability attitude has largely unhealthy consequences	**A bearability attitude has largely healthy consequences**
An unbearability attitude has largely unhealthy consequences because it tends to lead to UNEs, unconstructive behaviour and highly distorted and biased subsequent thinking when the person is facing an adversity.	A bearability attitude has largely healthy consequences because it tends to lead to HNEs, constructive behaviour and realistic and balanced subsequent thinking when the person is facing an adversity.

Appendix 5

Reasons why devaluation attitudes are false, illogical and have largely unhealthy consequences and unconditional acceptance attitudes are true, logical and have largely healthy consequences

Devaluation attitude	Unconditional acceptance attitude
A devaluation attitude is false	**An unconditional acceptance attitude is true**
When you hold a devaluation attitude in the face of your adversity, this attitude is based on the following ideas, which are all false:	When you hold an unconditional acceptance attitude in the face of your adversity, this attitude is based on the following ideas, which are all true:
<ul><li>A person (self or other) or life can legitimately be given a single global rating that defines their or its essence and the worth of a person or life is dependent upon conditions that change (e.g., my worth goes up when I do well and goes down when I don't do well).</li><li>A person or life can be rated on the basis of one of his or her or its aspects.</li></ul>	<ul><li>A person (self or other) or life cannot legitimately be given a single global rating that defines their or its essence, and their or its worth, as far as they or it have it, is not dependent upon conditions that change (e.g., my worth stays the same whether or not I do well).</li><li>Discrete aspects of a person and life can be legitimately rated, but a person or life cannot be legitimately rated on the basis of these discrete aspects.</li></ul>
Both of these ideas are false and thus your devaluation attitude is false.	Both of these ideas are true and thus your devaluation attitude is true.

A devaluation attitude is illogical	An unconditional acceptance attitude is logical
A devaluation attitude is based on the idea that the whole of a person or a life can logically be defined by one of their or its parts. Thus: ⊙ *'x is bad… and therefore I am bad.'* This is known as the part-whole error, which is illogical.	An unconditional acceptance attitude is based on the idea that the whole of a person or a life cannot be defined by one or more of their or its parts. Thus: ⊙ *'x is bad, but this does not mean that I am bad, I am a fallible human being even though x occurred.'* Here the part-whole illogical error is avoided. Rather it is held that the whole incorporates the part, which is logical.
A devaluation attitude has largely unhealthy consequences	**An unconditional acceptance attitude has largely healthy consequences**
A devaluation attitude has largely unhealthy consequences because it tends to lead to UNEs, unconstructive behaviour and highly distorted and biased subsequent thinking when the person is facing an adversity.	An unconditional acceptance attitude has largely healthy consequences because it tends to lead to HNEs, constructive behaviour and realistic and balanced subsequent thinking when the person is facing an adversity.

Appendix 6
ABCD Blank form with instructions

Situation =			
	'A' (Adversity) =		
'r/e B'	(rigid/extreme basic attitude) =	'f/n B'	(flexible/non-extreme basic attitude) =
'C'	(emotional consequence) =	'C'	(emotional goal) =
	(behavioural consequence) =		(behavioural goal) =
	(thinking consequence) =		(thinking goal) =

1. Write down a brief, objective description of the 'situation' you were in.
2. Identify your 'C' – your major disturbed emotion, your dysfunctional behaviour and, if relevant, your distorted subsequent thinking.
3. Identify your 'A' – this is what you were most disturbed about in the situation, known as an 'adversity' (Steps 2 and 3 are interchangeable.)
4. Set emotional, behavioural and thinking goals.
5. Identify your rigid/extreme basic attitudes ('r/e Bs'), i.e., rigid attitude + awfulising attitude, unbearability attitude or devaluation attitude.
6. Identify the alternative flexible/non-extreme attitudes ('f/n Bs') that will enable you to achieve your goals, i.e., flexible attitude + non-awfulising attitude, bearability attitude or unconditional acceptance attitude.
7. Develop persuasive arguments to convince yourself that your rigid/extreme attitudes are false, illogical and unhealthy, and that your flexible/non-extreme attitudes are true, logical and healthy – 'D'. These arguments will help you to achieve your emotional, behavioural and thinking goals.
8. Re-examine 'A' and consider how realistic it was. Given all the facts, would there have been a more realistic way of looking at 'A'? If so, write it down.

'D' (Dialectical examination of 'B'*)

Taking action

Re-examine 'A' =

Note: * Dialectical examination is a process of resolving a conflict between opposing views (e.g., rigid/extreme basic attitudes and flexible/non-extreme basic attitudes.

Index